ELEMENTS OF DESIGN

"Pure, unadulterated beauty should be the goal of civilization."
— Rowena Reed Kostellow

DESIGN BRIEFS |||||||||||||||| ESSENTIAL TEXTS ON DESIGN

PUBLISHED BY
PRINCETON ARCHITECTURAL PRESS
A MCEVOY GROUP COMPANY
202 WARREN STREET
HUDSON, NEW YORK 12534
WWW.PAPRESS.COM.

PROJECT EDITOR: JENNIFER N. THOMPSON
DESIGNERS: TUCKER VIEMEISTER; SETH KORNFELD
ROWENA REED KOSTELLOW FOUNDATION COMMITTEE: LOUIS NELSON (CHAIR); LEN BACICH; PETER BARNA; GINA CASPI; LINDA CELANTANO; GERALD GULOTTA; BRUCE HANNAH; KATE HIXON; DEBERA JOHNSON; RITASUE SIEGEL; LISA SMITH; WILLIAM FOGLER; TUCKER VIEMEISTER; BILL KATAVOLOS; CRAIG VOGEL; JAMES FULTON
PRODUCER: LOUIS NELSON

SPECIAL THANKS TO: NETTIE ALJIAN, ANN ALTER, NICOLA BEDNAREK, JANET BEHNING, MEGAN CAREY, PENNY CHU, JAN CIGLIANO, RUSSELL FERNANDEZ, CLARE JACOBSON, MARK LAMSTER, NANCY EKLUND LATER, LINDA LEE, JANE SHEINMAN, LOTTCHEN SHIVERS, KATHARINE SMALLEY, SCOTT TENNENT, AND DEB WOOD OF PRINCETON ARCHITECTURAL PRESS
—KEVIN C. LIPPERT, PUBLISHER

ALL IMAGES ARE FROM THE PRATT INSTITUTE INDUSTRIAL DESIGN DEPARTMENT ARCHIVES AND WERE PHOTOGRAPHED BY WILLIAM FOLGER, GERALD GULOTTA, IVAN RIGBY, OR OTHERS, EXCEPT AS NOTED BELOW:

25, INTERIORS; 43, I.D. MAGAZINE; 148T, COURTESY TUCKER VIEMEISTER; 148B, COURTESY MARLAN POLHEMUS; 149, HENRY DREYFUSS ASSOCIATES; 150TL, KNOLL; 150TR, TOTO; 150B, KENNETH WILLARDT; 151, KNOLL; 152T, COURTESY DON GENARO; 152BL, AUTOMOBILE CITROËN; 152, TIMOTHY HURSLEY; 153, DAN HOWELL; 154TR, DICK PATRICK; 154TL, KNOLL; 154B, ROBERT SOMERS; 155T, COURTESY GERALD GULOTTA; 155B, CUISINE COOKWARE; 156T, JEFF GOLDBERG; 156BL, MARK JOHNSTON; 156BR, ELLIOTT KAUFMAN; 157, GILLETTE

LIBRARY OF CONGRESS CATALOGING-IN-PUBLICATION DATA

HANNAH, GAIL GREET.
ELEMENTS OF DESIGN: ROWENA REED KOSTELLOW AND THE STRUCTURE OF VISUAL RELATIONSHIPS / BY GAIL GREET HANNAH.
152 P. : ILL. (SOME COL.) ; 22 CM. — (DESIGN BRIEFS)
ISBN 10: 1-56898-329-8 (PBK. : ALK. PAPER)
ISBN 13: 978-1-56898-329-5
1. DESIGN; 2. FORM PERCEPTION; 3. VOLUME PERCEPTION;
4. KOSTELLOW,
ROWENA REED. I. TITLE. II. SERIES.
NK1510.H286 2002
745.4'071'07471—DC21

2002002214

ELEMENTS OF DESIGN

ROWENA REED KOSTELLOW AND THE STRUCTURE OF VISUAL RELATIONSHIPS

BY GAIL GREET HANNAH

PRINCETON ARCHITECTURAL PRESS, NEW YORK

CONTENTS

PAOLA ANTONELLI

Curator of Architecture and Design,
The Museum of Modern Art, New York

PURE, UNADULTERATED AMERICAN BEAUTY

After decades of ideological suspicion, we at last feel again comfortable using the "b" word. It is a different kind of beauty, which has become human and immanent and is acknowledged to be in the eyes of billions of beholders. Pasionaria Rowena Kostellow's motto, which reinforces the supreme principle of beauty with attributes such as "pure" and "unadulterated" and contemplates it as a responsibility to people, carries the echo of a social mission that is centuries old. In her philosophy, beauty was a superior state to be attained through strenuous practice and progressive shedding of impurities, which could be attained only by the few privileged individuals who could devote their lives to it. Studying Ms. Kostellow's work is akin to taking a plunge into a different ancient time, when the elite's task was to produce beauty and then make it available to the masses.

The lucidity, both intellectual and formal, of her principle highlights a quintessential characteristic of American design. American design, like much of American culture, perennially oscillates between populism and elitism, between the revolutionary beauty and availability of Tupperware and the elusive exclusivity of Marcel Breuer's furniture. Both extremes express design excellence, in the design of the brand or the detailed perfection of one item. The long path toward a true American design has reflected this dichotomy, a by-product of the country's powerful class system.

Postmodern thinkers like Jaques Derrida, Betsey Johnson, and Pedro Almodóvar have taught us that beauty is all in the intention, the novelty, the composition, and the attitude, certainly not in such a reductive concept as formal homogeneity. The emancipation from the old-fashioned concept of "absolute beauty" is one of the greatest achievements of this century. The ideal of "style democracy" is a recurring theme in architecture and design.

Beauty today is a matter of composition and personality, in urban fashion, design, and architecture alike. Hip-hop music, based as it is on sampling and composing new and pre-existing tracks and giving them a finishing varnish of surprising novelty, is the paradigm recipe for contemporary beauty. It is based on synthesis and individual talent. Like music, fashion is a successful manifestation of democratic individualism in an end result called "style." Fashion demonstrates that beauty coincides today with the affirmation of personal taste and that individuals can and have been upgraded to the role of authors and sole arbiters.

Yet in the early 1800s, America was still psychologically a European colony that strove to emulate the refinement of the European aristocracy. Furniture for the wealthy was generally imported. The middle class longed for the same ideal of luxury and style, and bought imitations. The nineteenth-century Shakers provided one of the first examples of original American modern design. Their furnishings and interior architecture display a sobriety and honesty that are a direct portrayal of the circumstances that generated them. Materials were used in harmony with their capabilities, which American design historian Arthur Pulos calls "the principle of beauty as the natural by-product of functional refinement," a principle many use now to define goodness in design.

After Henry Ford's emblematic Model T experiment of the 1920s, the American 1950s came closest to this ideal. Those were the years when resources from the idle war industry were converted to civilian and domestic use by such great designers as Charles and Ray Eames and anonymous engineers to provide the booming middle class with a brand-new, clean, efficient and especially affordable world.

The East Coast architectural aristocracy, led by The Museum of Modern Art and Harvard University, had platonically embraced the visions of modernist émigrés Walter Gropius and Mies van der Rohe. The new architecture and design "for modern living" coming from the West and the Midwest were about practice, not theory, and were born out of economy. They were symbols of American sensibility and idealism.

Ms. Kostellow still studied the divine, absolute, and Nietzschean kind of beauty of European modernism. The European modernist ideal, she realized, no longer existed as an import and needed to be translated and assimilated into New World culture. During her passionate career as an educator, an aware first step in this longer democratic process, she gave her students a clear idea of the sublime and a path to achieve it. She empowered them toward future choices, to enrich a quintessentially American culture, and to free it from its European chains.

EMILIO AMBASZ

architect and designer
former Curator of Architecture and Design,
The Museum of Modern Art, New York

It is deeply regrettable I never had the pleasure of meeting Ms. Rowena Reed Kostellow, but from reading her former students' statements, I know that she must have been a most beguiling teacher. I would dare to call her a pedagogical seducer. It is obvious that she received every student's idea with great respect for the kernel of imagination it might have contained and made it bloom. She was both earth and rain.

I can imagine her observing a student's timid proposal, gleaning the chaff from the wheat, and inviting him to participate in that magical process whereby she turned that seed into the plant it might become. She taught by example. Shamans also teach that way.

Industrial design is an intellectual profession. In less label-oriented times, it would have been called a métier of arts and crafts, its ultimate product an artifact. It was one of her many gifts to never allow her students to forget that their apostolate is to be functional-form givers, to engage an act of creation that has to encompass both pragmatic and emotional considerations. One of the rigors that she taught was that meeting the operational requirements of a new product is a necessary but not a sufficient condition for its adopting a meaningful identity. The product has to represent a formal embodiment of spirit and intelligence; it has not only to talk to the mind but also to touch the heart. Else it would be a lifeless instrument, just useful to accomplish a purpose, but arid and without contribution to a well-rounded life.

Her manner of teaching, creating in front of the students, was not used to dazzle them, although I suspect that when she could dazzle herself, she felt uplifted. A through and through teacher, she did not hide the fact that the act of creation is a "lonely, frightening jump." The student has to jump alone, even if his/her hand is held until the last moment. But she taught them also that one could train for such a jump and revealed to them the mental processes she went through to arrive at her questions and suggestions. Eminently, she was concerned with bestowing a method upon each student to reduce seemingly disconnected problems into a systematic organization of relationships. In essence, she never forgot that *method* comes from that Greek word *methodos* ("the way").

Naturally, in our profession, using again a method that insured success before will fall short of meeting new needs. Therefore, in addition to teaching her students methods for cartographically taking stock of previous solutions to seemingly similar problems, she reminded them constantly that designers make maps for places that don't yet exist, that the empirical procedure of gathering past experience and the normative stage whereby goals are stated must culminate in a synthetic act of inventing forms that will satisfy all the needs—mental and emotional—of the user.

At the same time, I can't avoid suspecting that she fulfilled herself as a designer vicariously through her students. But since she was a very generous person, she didn't force them to adopt her images but guided them as she took them on a voyage through her spirit. I can't say all students were reborn, but in the cases of the gifted ones, they were transformed.

I hope readers of this book derive a sense of wonder at the splendid exercises that Ms. Kostellow could inspire her students to produce. Some of them are as delicate and poetically suggestive as a sculpture by Jean Arp. They reflect the design concerns and pursuits prevailing at the time. But this is irrelevant, as it is irrelevant when we can identify the period when a Brancusi or an Eames was created. These works are to this day still very moving.

It is, at the same time, melancholy to think where some of the gifted students, whose exercises are here illustrated, may be now. I take comfort from looking at the work of others who, less promising in school, revealed themselves later in the practice of their profession and have brought to full fruition her teachings.

This book is obviously a message of love from her students. Let's fancy that she can see it. I, for one, am touched by the love and recognition that her students wished to express. When they were with her, they might have thought her to be the more gifted one. Now they realize that loving her teachings so much has made them the richer ones. The generational transfer has been completed.

JUDY COLLINS

singer and songwriter

On a bright Sunday morning in the winter of 1983, I had a special date-brunch with Rowena Reed Kostellow, teacher and mentor of some of the most successful industrial designers in the world today. Rowena was my friend as well as being friend and teacher to my husband, Louis Nelson. That morning, he and I took a cab downtown to SoHo from our home on the Upper West Side of Manhattan. In the streets the light danced—I thought of Georgia O'Keefe and Edward Hopper, their sun-streamed walls, blossoms of color.

Rowena's loft was on the corner of Greene and Houston, down the street from the Puck building, whose red brick shimmered in the light. (Years later Rowena's friends would gather at the Puck to bid our final farewell to her, "Amazing Grace" and all.) This morning, like that of a precocious ten-year-old, Rowena's luminous face greeted us at the top of the long flight of stairs to her home on the first floor of the loft. It was chilly that morning and we hurried up the stairs. Rowena hugged us each in turn and beckoned us into her studio and home.

Rowena, at eighty-three, was tiny and wiry, with high cheekbones, dancing eyes, and a fine featured face, more alive and young than many at twenty. She had clearly been an unadulterated beauty in her youth, even though the years had drawn their mark upon her. It was as if her very person contained the essence of what she taught—the basis of fine art, architecture, and graphic and industrial design. "Make it beautiful," she said, and she was.

"Young is in the mind," she would say when people asked her why, in her eighties and retired from teaching at Pratt, she still taught her Saturday morning classes to a select group of devoted students. She wanted as much out of life as it had to offer and offered herself in an unstinting and complete way to her students until the day she died.

Settling in and shedding our coats, Louis and I looked around the room at Rowena's world, a loft full of soft, filtered morning light and the heavenly scent of quiche—baked by Rowena's hands. "It is so simple. I will show you how," she said. She had refused our invitation to take her out to the SoHo Charcuterie, where we had been together before. No, she said, this morning she would cook for us. There was steamed asparagus and rich coffee. "Delicious rocket fuel," she said. "I still drink the real thing."

Her loft was a model of practical magic: the purple irises we had brought she put in a simple glass vase to show off their color; the kitchen was simple stove top, and walk-around chopping and serving board, handy stools to pull up at the simple table, and room to stretch out nearby on a long couch and look at students work; her separate sleeping quarters were in the distance, discreetly closed off with a fall of faun fabric. The whole place was full of the softened New York light and the aroma of the quiche, the fresh-ground coffee. We ate, talking and laughing, finishing off our brunch with a raspberry tart—bought at Dean & Deluca, she admitted guiltily.

The morning shines with startling detail now, a gift from Rowena.

Rowena became my friend in 1978, the year I met Louis. Rowena had been his teacher at Pratt Institute in New York, where he graduated with a degree in industrial design in 1958. After a five-year stint in the army, where he became a captain and helicopter instructor, Louis went back to school for his master's degree at Pratt and became Rowena's assistant. By then Louis had established a friendship with his mentor that would last until her death, in 1988.

Louis and Rowena were close, talking often, visiting often. Rowena inspired Louis as she inspired so many of her students. After her death, a number of her students and friends started the Rowena Reed Kostellow Fund and asked Louis to chair the fund, the purpose being to furthur the understanding of the principles that guided Rowena's educational philosophy—the study of abstract three-dimensional relationships—in turn fostering the creation of objects and environments that are beautiful as well as functional.

Rowena became one of my girlfriends. We admired (and sometimes coveted!) each other's clothes, complimented one another's taste. We talked about the books we were reading, gossiped about our mutual friends—a group of designers and artists brought together by our lives and parties and dinners together—and delighted in one another's company. I knew Rowena had seen the world and knew the false from the real and the best from the good. And her fondness for my life partner, her appreciation for his gifts, was reassuring and told me I had made the greatest choice, for me, that I could make. I was delighted that Rowena approved of me, for, though I felt she was a girlfriend, she was older and, I knew, wise.

I admired Rowena for her own qualities even as I learned about much of her impact through the eyes of the people who had known and studied with her. There were students of hers in our lives, some of them our friends, like Bruce Hannah, Rita Sue Siegel, Mark Harrison, Jim Fulton, Gerry Gulotta, Tucker Viemeister, and Bill Katavalos, who went on to influence international design. They've passed on Rowena's vision to many whose work has made an impact on the things we use every day—our cars, our furniture, our coffeepots, our dishes, toasters, fabrics, buildings, toys, museums, jewelry, clothing, utensils. Rowena was a pioneer, and in my eyes, she had carved out, with her husband and mentor, Alexander Kostellow, a way to pass on her great gifts to her students.

I had had great teachers in my life and could appreciate Rowena's gifts and my husband's devotion to her. When Rowena spoke of line and continuity in design, she spoke in the same language my singing teacher Max Margulis used when he spoke of singing. He used different words, perhaps—such as *clarity* and *phrasing*—but he was mirroring Rowena's advice to "make it beautiful, make the line have a life of its own, let it not falter, halt, and miss the mark." Max could easily have used the same advice about the line of a phrase of music. "Go to the end of the phrase," Max might say. "Go to the end of the thought in the line. Complete the movement," might be the way Rowena would say it. Max was alive during my friendship with Rowena, and often they would talk together at our parties. My great piano teacher, Antonia Brico, would have fit in perfectly with Max and Rowena as she spoke of the phrasing of a line in Mozart or Chopin. "Don't abandon the phrase," Brico might say. "See it through to the end. Make it beautiful." Teachers after the same thing in completely different disciplines.

When I need to write songs or just to get my piano playing up to speed, I go back to basics, do runs and exercises, play Hanon and Czerny, limber up my fingers so that I may write a song or play a song well. When Louis is thinking about new ideas for his work or just freshening his "hand" for seeing, he often goes into his little studio in our home and, using the way he was taught by Rowena, forms miniature sculptures, lovely, fragile things that are like poetry in themselves, that use Rowena's concepts for the use of space—line, plane, and volume. These sculptures, done for the love of the concepts he has been taught, done to remind him of the basic tenets he learned from Rowena, remind me of the grace that permeates his "big" work as well—museum spaces, the Korean War Veterans Memorial Wall, the Dag Hammarschold Medal—or even some of my record covers. He goes back to the basics and, as Rowena taught, learns again to "make it beautiful."

We live with the work of many of Rowena's students in the world today, and sometimes we see a beautiful design that stuns us—an elegant line in an automobile, the shape of a beautifully designed utensil like Tucker Viemeister's garlic press, his sunglasses, a streamlined jet airplane, a comfortable couch, a Hannah chair, a truly beautiful building, or the mural at the Korean War Veterans Memorial. I often see my husband's annoyance at something that is not done with the beauty and usefulness he was taught.

That day in Rowena's loft, we spoke of such things, laughing at the inconsistencies, talking of solutions. Rowena's deep desire was to pass along her insight, her sense of the whole person, whose needs are artistic as well as utilitarian, physical as well as emotional.

When Rowena died at the age of eighty-eight, she left a cadre of students who have brought beauty and usefulness together in every conceivable kind of design. Many of these same students and colleagues came to bid her farewell, entering the doors of the Puck building, down the street from her loft, where for so many years Rowena lived, taught, and entertained with her intelligence, wit, and an occasional quiche. Her legacy, perpetuated by those who have gone out from her studio, like ships on the water, to all parts of the world, will continue to carry her essential teaching. Make it work, make it useful, and above all, make it beautiful!

ACKNOWLEDGMENTS

This book started in the mind of Ms. Reed many years ago. In 1964, as a returning graduate student at Pratt, I worked as her assistant. One of my jobs was to help organize the notes that she had been making for years on 5"x7" cards and putting in piles all around her office. Much later, in 1982, after I started my own office, she talked about wanting to get "the book" done, and I helped put together her proposal for a National Endowment for the Arts grant. She was always working on fine-tuning her ideas and methods with her students. Now she had a stipend to get the book started.

In September 1988, Ms. Reed left us after being in the hospital for a short time. I remember her saying when I visited her in the intensive care unit, "I'm so glad you came because I want to talk with you about something." It was about a student of hers. Never about herself. About a month or so after her death, I was asked to attend a meeting with Jim Fulton, Bruce Hannah, Harvey Bernstein, Tucker Viemeister, Lenny Bacich, Jeff Kapec, and Lisa Smith. We huddled around a table in a small coffee shop and decided to get Ms. Reed's book done. Published.

Jim and I met frequently with our friends at his office. There were many reminiscences. Early on, Jim suggested we start a foundation, the Rowena Reed Kostellow Fund, to perpetuate her standards of design and education and to help Pratt and all design students in their quest to make things beautiful. Jim, who was chair of Pratt's Board of Trustees, suggested it be housed at Pratt because it would be easier to administer, and we could have total control of how the fund would be used. It was suggested that I be the fund's chairperson. I asked RitaSue Siegel to join us. She was a dear friend of Rowena's and one of her students. She knew the profession in detail, enjoyed singular respect amongst its leaders, and has been at every committee meeting, giving selflessly of her time and knowledge.

Others would come. Some would go—Ruth Shuman, Sandra Longyear Richardson, Sandy Weisz—each giving as s/he could.

The mainstay of the fund was always there and always in attendance and always ready to help at the various functions, awards ceremonies, and fund-raisers: Jim, Bruce, Tucker, Lisa, Linda, Gerry, RitaSue, and Gail.

Bruce Hannah, then chair of the Department of Industrial Design, was a special creative force in the early years and provided access to the archives of the department for this book. With great caring he helped at every moment during his busy professional and educational schedule. Peter Barna and Debera Johnson continued in the same spirit after Bruce left the chair position.

This extraordinary book is the result of many yet, as we all know in things like this, produced by the hard work of a special dedicated few. I asked Gail Greet Hannah to write the book. She had written a special bio of Ms. Reed for

Industrial Design Magazine and knew the design profession more than intimately. She spent countless hours researching and interviewing many who knew Rowena—all without pay or reimbursement of expenses, not requesting any royalty. Any monies from the sale of the book will go to the Rowena Fund. Tucker Viemeister directed the book's design, again without any remuneration, and Seth Kornfeld produced the handsome design. Gerald Gulotta, Tucker, Linda Celenatano, and Gina Caspi led a long and detailed process of photo editing.

Lisa Smith agreed to be executive director of the fund and has directed our annual events, gathering the forces needed to bring each to successful closure. Giovanni Pellone and Brigitte Means have donated their design services for the flyers and other material that the fund has published over the years.

Mackarness Goode, formerly vice president for institutional development at Pratt, provided invaluable guidance, support, and patience over the years. His predecessors, Mary Steel and Robert Fricker, were helpful indeed. Dr. Tom Schutte, President of Pratt Institute, has been highly supportive, providing creative suggestions for the betterment of the fund, the perpetuation of Rowena's memory, and how we could help Pratt's industrial design students.

Among the special donors who have supported the development of this book are Pamela Waters and Midori Imatake. The book has also benefited from the unrestricted donations of RitaSue Siegel, Blanche Bernstein, Gerry Gulotta, and many others.

I am indebted to a few friends in the publishing business for their advice and assistance during this process— Loretta Barrett, Mitchell Ivers, and Jim Truelove—to the many comments from other editors and publisher, and to Jennifer Thompson at Princeton Architectural Press, who was instrumental in the publishing of this work.

It doesn't seem like such a length of time has passed since starting this journey. We wanted to get the book completed quickly. I thank everyone for his patience. I believe the wait was worth it.

Mostly, I am thankful to Ms. Reed, for giving of her life and soul to her profession and to her students and to me. One was always fearful at a Ms. Reed crit. I hope she approves of this book.

Louis Nelson
Chair
Rowena Reed Kostellow Fund

INTRODUCTION

Rowena Reed Kostellow taught design for half a century. She was an immensely influential teacher who spent her life developing and refining a methodology for teaching what she called the "structure of visual relationships" underlying all art and design. The principles of study that she helped formulate were embodied in a foundation curriculum that became the basic, universal first year of study for all Pratt Institute art and design students. Foundation studies, strongly influenced by the Pratt curriculum, were adopted in schools of art and design throughout the country. In many schools, as at Pratt, they are still the bedrock upon which advanced, specialized studies in the arts are built.

But the content of that study has become diluted over time, and there is less consensus about what should be taught and how. There are several reasons for this. Formalisms of all kinds have long been in decline, and one of the results has been a predictable loss of rigor in foundation (principle-based) approaches. The number of instructors educated and interested in teaching this complex curriculum has declined. The current focus in education in general on preparing students for success in the marketplace has encouraged the inclination to skip anything that does not seem immediately relevant to the real world and the global economy. And technology has changed the way we think about and practice art and design. Painting and sculpture have been with us for millennia. Now the computer and video media offer tools with which we are able to explore the fourth dimension of time and motion, and present new creative opportunities along with increased complexity.

Computer-aided design was on the horizon by the end of Rowena Reed's life, although it had yet to transform design practice in the way we now take for granted. She was especially concerned about the impact of the computer on the practice of three-dimensional design and cautioned against using the computer to do things that she believed only the human eye and hand could do. It now remains for those who value her approach to design education to make the intellectual leap and to devise new ways to integrate these new opportunities and new modes of expression with the traditional 2-D/3-D creative process.

In the meantime, a valuable legacy is being lost. Rowena Reed had the unshakable conviction that foundation studies aimed at exploring abstract visual relationships are essential to creating and appreciating art and design. She focused her own attention and considerable gifts on exploring these relationships in the three-dimensional realm. She left a body of knowledge, most of it oral, that begs to be captured before it disappears.

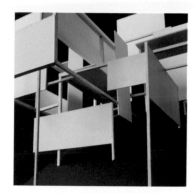

"Rowena was very clear about the difference between 2-D and 3-D," explains William Fasolino, who directs Pratt's Foundation Program. "Three-dimensional objects are all around us, but we don't understand three dimensions. You need different muscles to push and pull and make something that's three-dimensional. Rowena's courses had that kind of flesh and blood. We've lost that."

In 1982, Reed was awarded an NEA grant to write a book on her structured approach to the study of visual relationships. She planned to document her methodology by defining and illustrating the vocabulary and carefully sequenced exercises at its heart. She did not live long enough to carry out her project. Shortly after her death, a group of former students and colleagues created the Rowena Reed Kostellow Fund to provide a source of support for the advancement of education in three-dimensional design and visual communications. One means for accomplishing this goal was to ensure that Reed's book become a reality.

Although she did not leave a detailed written record of her principles and methods, she did spend a lifetime talking about and demonstrating them, inside and outside the classroom, to students, colleagues, practicing professionals, and friends. This book documents her methodology by reconstructing her ongoing conversation from the recollections and notes of those who taught and studied with her, and from audio and visual tapes made in the last decade of her life.

The book includes a description of all the three-dimensional foundation experiences that she taught in the last thirty years of her career, plus some advanced three-dimensional exercises and her signature exercises in space analysis. Wherever possible, the book is illustrated with slides of work done by Rowena's students in classes taught by her. Where such slides were not available, exercises are illustrated with slides from classes taught by her colleagues and former students.

Although I have attempted to faithfully record Rowena's ideas and to capture her distinctive voice, it is impossible to reproduce the experience of being and working in her classroom. The essence of Rowena Reed's teaching was the experience itself. In fact, she called the exercises in her courses "experiences" because they led students to insight through intense, in-the-moment concentration, discovery, and revelation. They were powerful, personal epiphanies that finally defy description.

Many people offered hours of their time in interviews, extended conversations, and intellectual and moral support. Some of their voices are heard in this book. Others are not, but their recollections and insights inform every page. My heartfelt thanks to all of you. Special thanks to members of the Rowena Reed Kostellow Fund book committee: James Fulton, Bruce Hannah, Louis Nelson, RitaSue Siegel, and Tucker Viemeister, and to others who shared their notes and tapes, read the manuscript, made valuable suggestions and corrections, and pored through the visual record—especially Len Bacich, Gina Caspi, Linda Celentano, Bill Fogler, Gerry Gulotta, Kate Hixon, Debera Johnson, Jeff Kapec, Bill Katavolos, and Craig Vogel.

(A note on names: Rowena Reed Kostellow was known by several variations on her name by different people at different times in her life. In formal correspondence and official documents she was Rowena Reed Kostellow. In the professional world, she was known both as Rowena Reed Kostellow and Rowena Reed. In the classroom, she was called "Miss Reed" by students in the early years of her teaching career and then both "Miss Reed" and "Rowena" in later years. All variations are used in this book, since people are quoted using the name by which they knew her.)

Rowena Reed was interested in—one might say consumed by—the study of three-dimensional abstraction. She pursued it as an intriguing mystery in itself and as a means to an end. It was her mission to educate artists and designers by sensitizing their eyes and developing their powers of visual discrimination—she called it "visual literacy"—so that they would be inspired and prepared to make the world more beautiful. She laid out that goal with utter sincerity and the absolute conviction that it was the most important thing one could do with one's life.

The goal of this book is to document Rowena Reed's legacy for present and future generations, to honor that legacy through the words and work of artists and designers who built on it, and to pay tribute to an extraordinary woman and teacher, whose influence far exceeds the recognition she has enjoyed.

Gail Greet Hannah

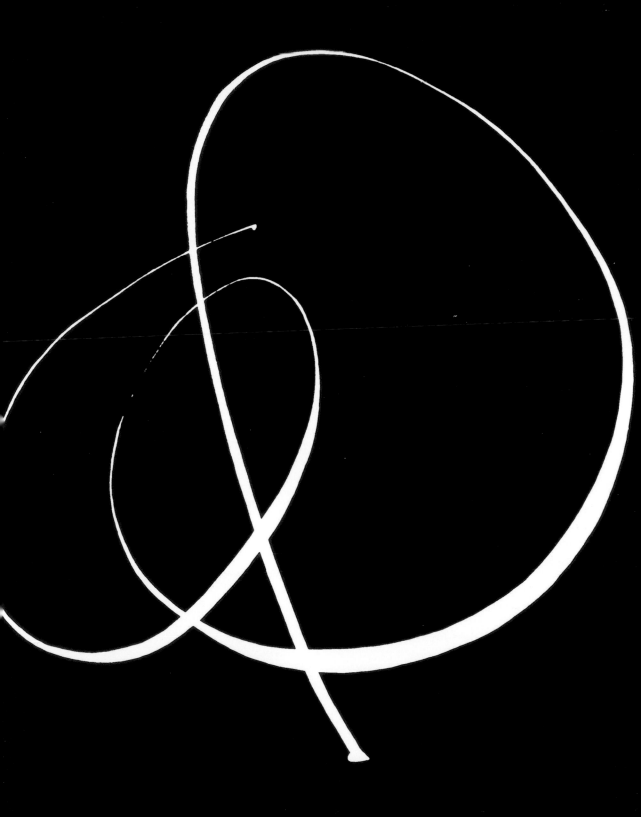

PART I
LIFE AND TIMES

The story of Rowena Reed Kostellow's life and work is inseparable from the story of American design educa-tion. She was present at the creation in 1934 of the country's first industrial design department, at Carnegie Technical Institute. She came to Pratt two years later to help found the department in which she taught for fifty years, and she continued to teach private classes until just weeks before she died. Hers was a household name within the industrial design profession, but she left an equally important legacy in the students who established and taught in industrial design departments throughout the country and passed on her principles and methods in their own teaching.

Rowena taught two generations of teachers following her husband's death, enlarging the circle of influence. Through her students-turned-educators, she made an enduring imprint on the teaching and practice of industrial design not only in the U.S. but beyond. Gerald Gulotta taught foundation principles in Guadalajara, Mexico; Craig Vogel applied them successfully in New Zealand; Cheryl Akner-Koler teaches them in the Department of Industrial Design at the University College of Art, Crafts and Design in Stockholm, Sweden.

Those who studied with Rowena didn't easily forget her. Although she was a small-boned woman of medium height who rarely raised her voice, she was a person of commanding presence and demanded enormous effort from her students. Abstraction doesn't come easily to most fledgling designers, but she insisted that an understanding of abstract visual order was at the heart of good design and that by perseverance and hard work, students could master that order. She refined a methodology for teaching that led students step by step to an understanding of and ability to use what she called the "structure of abstract visual relationships."

The first generation of educators studied with both Rowena and her husband, Alexander Kostellow, considered by many to be the father of American industrial design education. That generation included Marc Harrison, at the Rhode Island School of Design; James Henkle, at the University of Oklahoma; Robert Redman, at the University of Bridgeport; Jay Doblin, at the Institute of Design in Chicago; James Pirkl and Lawrence Feer, at Syracuse University; Ronald Beckman, at Cornell; Nelson Van Judah, at San Jose State University; Read Viemiester and Budd Steinhilber, at the Dayton Institute of Art; Bernard Stockwell, at the Columbus College of Art and Design; Jayne Van Alstyne, at Montana State University; Robert W. Veryzer, at Purdue University; Charles W. Smith, at the University of Washington; Robert McKim, at Stanford University; Carl Olsen and Homer Legasy, at the School for Creative Studies in Detroit; and Joseph Parriott, Giles Aureli, Gerald Gulotta, and Lucia DeRespinis, at Pratt.

THE EARLY YEARS

Rowena Reed was born in Kansas City, Missouri, on July 6, 1900. One of three children of a doctor and his wife, she grew up in a prominent family, in a growing heartland city, in the optimistic early years of a new century. Her upbringing gave her an unshakable confidence and sense of entitlement that never left her. She entered the University of Missouri in 1918, intending to study art. "I didn't know about three-dimensional design. I just took all the art courses I could take until there were no more," she recalled in an interview in 1982. "But even then, in my untrained way, I knew I was wasting my time. They weren't teaching me anything. There was no order, no organization, no continuity, nothing you could build on." She majored in journalism, worked for a while as a fashion illustrator and, in 1922, enrolled in the Kansas City Art Institute.

There she met Alexander Kostellow, a Persian-born, European-educated artist who was beginning his teaching career as an instructor in painting. She was his student. He was, she said, "simply the most interesting man I'd ever met."

Kostellow was a powerful personality. A graduate of the University of Berlin, with degrees in philosophy and psychology, he declined an invitation to join the German army during World War I and escaped the country through Holland, where he boarded a boat to the U.S. He jumped ship in Boston Harbor to avoid immigration officials, worked his way to New York, and studied for several years at the Art Students' League, the New York School of Fine and Applied Arts, and the National Academy of Design.

Kostellow felt the same way about his art education that Rowena Reed felt about her own. In 1947, he wrote: "My own experiences as an art student had not been too happy, because of the rather haphazard way one had to

Rowena Reed's 3-D design class

acquire the necessary knowledge and experience to become self-supporting in the field of art. Many of my fellow students were armed with plenty of patience and visions of ultimate glory, and spent years drawing casts in the national academies. Clearly it was a case of "life is short; art is long." But to one who looked upon the graphic and plastic arts as a legitimate profession and part of our economic setup, and expected a definite type of fundamental training as a preparation for his career, the method was far from satisfactory."*

Rowena Reed and Alexander Kostellow were married in Kansas City, and she returned with him to New York. There she studied sculpture with Alexander Archipenko. "I got a great deal from him," she said. "His work is very profound and beautifully organized, but after I studied for a while, I came to feel that the one thing lacking in his work was an awareness of space." That quest was to remain a driving force in her professional life.

In 1929, the couple moved to Pittsburgh, Pennsylvania, where Kostellow had been hired to teach painting at the Carnegie Technical Institute. Rowena taught at a private school and worked as a sculptor. She and Alexander had a daughter, Adele, their only child, and together they pursued their interest in developing a structured language for understanding and teaching visual arts.

INVENTING INDUSTRIAL DESIGN EDUCATION

In 1933, Rowena went to Europe to study and spent a year on the continent immersing herself in painting and sculpture. She returned to a bustling, industrious city. Pittsburgh was the very heart of the steel industry, and despite the depression that ravaged much of the country, chimneys belched, machines bellowed, business hummed. And there were new currents in the air.

Chris Freas takes a close look during one of Rowena Reed's Saturday class.

*"Industrial Design at Pratt Institute," in *Interiors,* July 1947

A decade earlier, American industry had begun to turn to specialists in the arts for help in designing and marketing products that would appeal to a growing audience of potential consumers. By the early 1930s, a small cadre of designers had emerged, Walter Dorwin Teague, Raymond Loewy, Henry Dreyfuss, Donald Deskey, Gilbert Rohde, Norman Bel Geddes, John Vassos, and Donald Dohner among them. These pioneers were staking out a new field, laying the groundwork for what would become the industrial design profession.

Dohner taught at Carnegie Tech. One day he was approached by an executive from Westinghouse, where he was a consultant, and, as Rowena Reed told the story, "The man said, 'We have something out there in the plant that we don't quite know what to do with. It's a new material, and we want some ideas about how to use it.' Well, Donald Dohner went out to look, and he saw big steel rollers with a rather innocuous material coming off them in sheets. First he said, 'Let's color it,' so they created beautiful Mondrian-like reds, yellows, and blues, which made the material much more appealing. Then he said, 'Let's spin it,' so they spun some trays—beautiful contemporary trays that people would be delighted to buy. After a while, they made them deeper and added a few bowls and other simple shapes. The material was the melamine plastic stuff that now covers all of our homes and all of our lives. They called it 'Micarta.'"

Dohner's experience convinced Kostellow that the opportunities in American industry were there for the taking. The time had come to formalize design training for a new design discipline. He had already spent years experimenting with ways to bring focus and order to art education and gaining direct experience as a design consultant to several firms in the area. So he and Dohner went to the Carnegie Tech administration and proposed the establishment of a degree-granting program in industrial design. They successfully argued their case, and in 1936, the Department of Industrial Design, the first of its kind in the United States, graduated its first students.

The industrial design experiment opened a new world for Rowena Reed. It fired her imagination and focused her interest on three-dimensional design. In 1938, she became formally involved in the design venture. Donald Dohner had been invited to Pratt Institute in 1934 by Dean James Boudreau to establish an industrial design department there. Dohner persuaded Kostellow to follow him to Brooklyn to develop the curriculum and teach courses in color and design. He asked Rowena to teach abstraction. Of their early work at Pratt, Arthur Pulos writes: "With Alexander Kostellow representing the philosophical, Rowena Reed the aesthetic, and Dohner the practical, they laid the triangular foundation for Pratt's program in industrial design."*

They were joined by Frederick Whiteman, Robert Kolli, Ivan Rigby, and Rolph Fjelde, and soon after by Eva Zeisel and Victor Canzani.

"In the beginning it was so great because we all spoke the same language," Rowena recalled. "It was awfully exciting. We were young and inconsiderate—the only way to get things done."

Their first big accomplishment was the development of a curriculum of study for all first year students in the art school. It was called, appropriately, "foundation" and was the first course of its kind specifically designed to address the requirements of the American art student and American society. It grew out of Kostellow's own experiences with pictorial structure and organizing the axes on the canvas, and out of Reed's experiments with visual organization in three dimensions. It became the prototype for foundation programs in many other schools across the country.

Alexander Kostellow in
Interiors magazine

*Arthur Pulos, *The American Design Adventure, 1940–1975*, MIT Press, 1988, p.166

Alexander Kostellow described the intention of the program: "The goal was to supply students not with disjointed bits of information but rather with an organized approach to the mechanics of design and the necessary inner discipline to carry out assigned problems...to develop an understanding of the elements of design, of structure, of the organizational forces which control them, and an ability to apply this knowledge to a variety of situations in designing for self-expression or for industry."

The program was general in its approach to the visual disciplines because, Kostellow wrote, "experience proves that specialized courses in design, like other programs devoted to the development of technical skills, restrict the esthetic potential of the student. Practical approaches rarely bring forth creative designers of importance. At best they produce skilled technicians."

Alexander Kostellow and Dean James Boudreau

Frederick Whiteman, who taught 2-D courses in the foundation year, saw foundation studies filling a vacuum that the academy itself had created. "Under the old apprentice system students could work on parts of a work, but only the master could put it together," he declared. "The commercial art schools took away the master. Now all students were drawing fragments, but they never learned to put it together. That is, they never learned to design. Foundation taught how it all went together."

Three years after Kostellow and Dohner established the industrial design department at Carnegie Tech, the New Bauhaus opened in Chicago. Mies van der Rohe moved it to IIT in 1938, where it later became the Institute of Design within the Illinois Institute of Technology. Directed by Laszlo Moholy-Nagy, the New Bauhaus promoted the course of study established by Walter Gropius at the original Bauhaus.*

Years later, when the foundation program was in full swing and attracting attention throughout the design community, Kostellow described his approach in detail in an article for *Interiors* magazine (July 1947):

We decided to start with the simplest and clearest elements of design and structure. From the primitive's point of view, but using the language of today, we aimed at establishing definite meanings by converting moods into terms, and by regarding each graphic and plastic element in the light of the student's own empathic and rhythmic reactions and sensory perceptions based on his personal experiences....Abstract conceptions and inner compulsions expressed in terms of graphic and plastic

*The Bauhaus was founded in 1919 by Gropius in Weimar, Germany. Its goal was to develop a modern architecture that embraced every aspect of life. Bauhaus methodology was based on a workshop approach. Its basic course of study was intended to break down the barriers separating architecture, applied art and technology in order to bridge the gulf between art and industrial production. (See Jurgen Joedicke, *A History of Modern Architecture*, Praeger, 1959.)

elements are stressed; experiments in creative expression rather than in techniques are encouraged.

For practical purposes, we have defined the word 'design' as a creative intent expressed graphically or plastically in terms of materials and manipulative processes, conditioned by a functional purpose, even when purely esthetic in its nature. It is an idea capable of graphic materialization. It is the art of merging an idea and feeling with concrete materials, so that the essential concept is inseparable from its material embodiment.

The component elements of this material embodiment are (1) line, (2) plane (or surface), (3) volume (positive and negative space), (4) value (light and dark), (5) texture, and (6) color. These are all the concrete elements the designer has at his disposal. Different materials...may to some extent affect these elements by introducing a variety of tactile and associative responses; but they never change the inherent qualities of these elements.

Before the student attempts to organize them, which really means manipulate them with an end purpose in view, he must learn through investigation and experimentation the functional capabilities of each of these elements. These are given in the form of individual problems.

To telescope as much experience as possible into a short time, we had to eliminate the types of problems which are primarily designed to achieve manipulative proficiency. We introduced power tools and machinery to avoid the somewhat therapeutic quality of handicraft.

We adapted, and in many cases established, a nomenclature of definite meaning to student and teacher alike. We agreed on a minimum standard for the evaluation of the student's work. This criterion is not based upon the teacher's preferences or taste, but on the amount of progress which the student achieves in the direction of self-expression. As much as possible we also broke down the barriers between the various courses, because we found it increasingly difficult to stay within the confines of one aspect of art training. This prevented the student from keeping his various experiences neatly tabulated in separate mental compartments for uses with different teachers on different problems.

In many cases it took quite a bit of ingenuity to devise the type of problem that would give the student the freedom of an imaginative approach, and upon its solution, would yield definite knowledge and control of a specific phase in designing.

In his study of the controlling forces of organization the student discovers that the mere proximity of plastic and graphic elements, or even a realistic grouping, will not produce an inner organizational coherence; that the title of an organization does not necessarily imply the possible content or impact; that a still life of cabbages by Bracque has far more esthetic significance than a battle scene by Messionier; that a simple Greek *kantharos* ("drinking cup") has more dignity and esthetic appeal than some national hero's statue done in flying stone draperies. And that the *Aspiring Bird,* an abstract shape by Brancusi, is far more monumental than a tortured marble on a pedestal of granite.

In the effort to achieve an organic entity, the student must transpose the world about him into symbols of his expression, using forces analogous to the ones which he finds in nature, e.g., balance, not the symmetrical equalization of weight or median lines, but the dynamic distribution of it to achieve livingness; tension, the awareness of the drama of existing relationships in space between widely separated parts of his organization; integration of positive and negative volumes, which invariably demands a readjustment of the purely representative forms; opposition, the forceful relationship of the heterogenous elements in the design structure; rhythm, the major motive of movement throughout the organization, whether it be expanding or repetitive in its nature; lines of continuation, the organo-dynamic thread of continuity within the structure; also some elementary evaluations, which in their application become synonymous with organizational forces, such as abstract equivalents, either as paths of vision, or as the total sum of visual forms.

The Pratt and Bauhaus foundation programs were similar in some ways. Both approaches were rooted in common intellectual and artistic assumptions. Their methodologies drew on modern scientific method and applied it to teaching the fundamentals of art making. They identified elements such as line, shape, form, space and color and systematically investigated each one. Students were expected to have a thorough understanding of the parts before attempting a completed work of art or design.**

Both approaches shifted the focus of aesthetic development and teaching to the solving of aesthetic problems. The reason for arranging forms or shapes was taken out of the religious, metaphysical, or moral sphere, and placed squarely in the perceptual one. And both proposed that there could be more than one correct solution to a problem—in opposition to the classic academic notion—and that such solutions required the nurturing of personal inspiration and individual talent.

In its practical agenda, the Bauhaus attempted to reconcile the aesthetic insights of the artist, the quality workmanship of the craftsman, and the technological advances of the machine. It declared that the artist should design in conjunction with the machine or for the machine. Although Kostellow's program was not interested in the crafts, it shared the Bauhaus goal to educate designers for an industrial, machine-driven economy.

But there were differences between the two approaches. Kostellow declared: "The introduction of 'die neue Sachlichkeit,' the clarification of functional design, was the closest to an organized approach I had yet encountered. But for what we wanted to accomplish at Pratt Institute, it lacked compactness and basic integration, it possessed some contradictory elements and in many instances indulged in too lengthy and pragmatic experimentation for experimentation's sake." And in response to the Bauhaus dictum that form follows function, he declared, "I have never agreed with the premise that function as such gives birth to esthetic expression. I feel that function is an expression of a time and that esthetic reactions influence man-made form, and we in turn are influenced by them."

This argument was key to Rowena Reed's point of view. She was adamant about the primacy of the visual and aesthetic aspects of design. She defined aesthetic expression as the designer's raison d'être.

The Bauhaus approached the study of form from the perspective of architecture. Kostellow came at it from a different point of view. "Alexander Kostellow was aware of the Bauhaus early on when it was still engaged in diverse experiments and was very dynamic," explains Craig Vogel. "The stuff was in the air before he left Europe. But he spoke a much wider avant-garde language than the Bauhaus. He was dealing with spatial perspectives. The difference was that Alexander wanted to start a design program, Gropius wanted to start an architecture program, and Mies (who succeeded Moholynagy at IIT) was even more reductive than Gropius. For him, everything flowed from architecture—and that was not what Alexander had in mind.

Vogel continues, "Alexander was closer to Peter Behrens, the father of corporate design." (Behrens, a German architect, designed several influential early modern buildings, including the AEG Turbine factory in Berlin in 1909. He was one of the first to develop an architecture for industrial buildings based on function and structural character, and the first artist to take on the whole range of corporate design, from identity to building fixtures.) Behrens's work was cut off by World War I, so he was probably not well known to Kostellow, who left Europe at the start of the war.

**The discussion of Bauhaus educational theory is indebted to Andrew Phelan,
"The Bauhaus and Studio Art Education," *Art Education*, September 1981

"Kostellow said, 'There's more manufacturing here than you can shake a stick at, and it's totally undisciplined.' Like Behrens, he wondered how to give technology a face—and that's still the big question in design today."

The debate about the relationship between industrial design education and architecture that heated up in the 1940s pitted the Gropius and Bauhaus-based camp, which supported the teaching of industrial design in schools of architecture, against design advocates who saw it more logically taught in schools of art. Donald Dohner defended the latter position for Pratt, and his argument won the day.*

There was another essential difference. "Alexander and Rowena introduced the consideration of space, as distinguished from just objects, as an important element in three-dimensional design," explains Richard Welch, who taught foundation courses at Pratt for more than a quarter century. "The Bauhaus was more interested in the object."

The differences in educational methodology between the two approaches were not all rooted in philosophy. There was also a radically different understanding of the American context. Kostellow, like Gropius, was rooted in a European perspective, but he held an advantage over the German architect in that he had come earlier to this country and he enthusiastically embraced American culture. He lived in large cities, but he also traveled and worked in the Midwest. (Frederick Whiteman says Kostellow ended up in Kansas City after he was thrown off a train for gambling.) He was open to American experience. He liked the spirit of the place, and he understood how it worked. Ronald Beckman, who studied with Reed and Kostellow at Pratt in the fifties and now directs the industrial design program at Syracuse University, observes: "Kostellow was not just German. He was also Persian. He was brought up to be comfortable with ambiguity and differences, and to manipulate the ambiguity. America is the most ambiguous place in the world, and he loved it."

Finally, unlike the Bauhaus, Kostellow approached the challenge of educating industrial designers as a social experiment. He saw art schools filled with talented, enthusiastic young people who needed to earn their livelihoods, and he knew there were few artists slated for greatness (or solvency) among them. It was a matter of supply and demand. Here was the talent—ready, willing, and capable of being made able—and there was industry, turning out a steady stream of formally inept products. These young artists could help. They could make a difference in the quality of life for everyone and make a decent living in the bargain. He created a program to make it happen.

*At least for a time. Design search firm principal RitaSue Siegel notes that in the last twenty-five years, there has been a strong impetus to move design programs out of art schools and into design schools or, as an alternative, into schools of architecture or engineering.

CREATING A COMMUNITY

The years from 1938 until Alexander Kostellow's death in 1954 were a time of extraordinary cohesiveness in Pratt's foundation program and growing industrial design department. Reed and Kostellow presided over a true intellectual and artistic community—people of like minds working together toward a common goal. Their apartment in Forest Hills, Queens, was a gathering place for teachers and students. Colleagues often joined them for weekends at their house near the western New Jersey–Pennsylvania border, where Alexander enjoyed cooking for their guests. The shared intellectual commitment and cooperative teaching practice that bound the community together provided a remarkable learning experience.

Ivan Rigby, Rowena Reed, Robert Koli, and Victor Canzani

"The secret was in the synergy, the simultaneity," explains Ron Beckman. "You took a battery of courses in two- and three-dimensional design, and the work in one class reinforced what you were doing in other classes. In 2-D design, you began drawing simple things in line while in 3-D Rowena would have you working in wire—it was the same line in three dimensions. In nature study, you might go to the Museum of Natural History and sketch animals on paper. Then in 3-D, you'd make three-dimensional sketches of animals, and the 2-D teacher would have you make drawings of the abstract equivalent of animals in line. Meanwhile, Alexander was giving color lectures to lay the theoretical foundation, and Dean Boudreau was lecturing on art history and the use of color in the art of Giotto and Rembrandt. The synchronized, simultaneous, reinforced learning experience was the secret. Years later, synergistics got into the lexicon of science, but Alexander Kostellow recognized early on that experience was holistic, not episodic."

The industrial design department flourished and continued to train designers throughout the Second World War. In fact, Kostellow set up special programs to prepare design students to aid the war effort. Joseph Parriott, who graduated in 1942 and returned to teach for and head the Department of Industrial Design in 1966, recalls the war years: "Kostellow understood that the kind of thinking ID students were doing at Pratt was essential to certain parts of the service. In 1940, as the war heated up, he set up a fantastic program in camouflage for those of us carrying draft cards. I was designing from the minute I went into the Corps of Engineers. In Paris, I met up with Ivan Rigby and Robert Kolli, who were working on the models for the Normandy landing and the Rhine river crossing. We all took our design training right through the war."

In the decade between 1945 and 1955, Pratt industrial design got a terrific boost of energy from World War II and Korean War veterans returning to school on the GI Bill. These older, highly ambitious students were smart, focused, and had life experience. Some of them had families living in temporary barracks on the library lawn. They attacked their schoolwork with no-nonsense energy and an eye on the prize. Their mere presence could be tough for other students, many of them teenage kids just out of high school. Designer and publisher James Fulton recalls the late forties: "Wide-eyed and bushy tailed on the first day of school, I walked into a design class, and a twenty-eight-year-old captain out of the Air Corps sat down next to me. It was daunting. These guys had a tremendous reservoir of talent."

By 1953, the Pratt program in industrial design had gone from a three-year certificate course of study to a four-year degree program. Kostellow was head of the department, and he added courses in humanities, the "technics of civilization," and social and economic studies. He believed that the best designer is a well-read, culturally and historically sophisticated person prepared to bring an informed perspective to the work.

Gerald Gulotta and Student

He also believed that the industrial designer had to be a realist. He did not want to train designers "who tend to look over the marketplace rather than belong to it," and he believed industry should be a participating factor.

He collaborated with a number of leading companies in the U.S. to establish and equip Pratt's Experimental Design Laboratory and work on mutual projects. Participating companies included producers of basic materials, such as Monsanto Chemicals (Plastics Division) and Reynolds Metals; large distributors, such as Sears and Roebuck and Shell Oil; and manufacturers, such as the Elgin National Watch Company, Gorham Silver, and E.A. Electrical Laboratories. Member companies had workroom offices on campus and sent staff designers on a rotating basis to advise student projects and help with independent research.

At midcentury, Pratt was one of the premier design schools in the world. Its graduating students were being snapped up by industry as well as starting firms of their own. Others were going on to found and teach in industrial design departments across the country and around the globe. Rowena and Alexander were the center of the circle.

"They were very different but complementary," says William Katavolos, professor of architecture at Pratt, who studied with Kostellow and, in the 1960s, taught with Rowena in the industrial design department. "When Rowena and Alexander were teaching side by side, I don't think there was another school in the country that could equal it. If you studied with them both, you got a broad education. His lectures were extraordinary—never a boring moment. You'd get into color reversals, and he'd drag in Newton. Rowena couldn't lecture like that, but I never saw Alexander give a crit like Rowena could. There was romantic conflict. It was Arthurian."

"I think there was a balance between them, between the aesthetic and the functional, similar to the balance between Ray and Charles Eames," Craig Vogel says. "I think Alexander owned the mind of it—the logical system—but Rowena owned the soul."

In the summer of 1954, Reed and Kostellow went to Detroit to work on the design of the General Motors Frigidaire "Kitchen of the Future." While in Detroit, Kostellow suffered a heart attack and died. He was fifty-eight years old.

BORN ABSTRACT

"Alexander Kostellow was a juggler, a genius at keeping all the balls in the air," Ron Beckman says. "Rowena Reed only juggled one ball, but she could do everything with it." Three-dimensional form making was Rowena Reed's magnificent obsession, and after the death of her partner in life and work, she took the study of three-dimensional abstraction into an entirely new realm.

"Kostellow created the foundation course in three-dimensional visual abstraction, which Rowena Reed considered key, based on years of his own study of the abstract intelligence of the best of western art and design," explains William Fogler, who studied with Reed and Kostellow at Pratt and became one of the first of many former students to join the industrial design faculty. "In contrast, the advanced courses in visual abstraction created by her were based only on her, on what she saw. His contribution was eclectic; it embraces the best insights to be found in western art. Her contribution was egocentric; it glows with the insight of one majestically gifted woman. Alexander Kostellow explained the difference. He said, 'It took me many years to learn abstraction. Miss Reed was born abstract.'"

"She wasn't directly connected intellectually or professionally to anyone," says Fogler. "She disconnected from her husband, the constructivists, European design. She was a terribly complex person—and very original. The meaning of her insight is that a three-dimensional object or space cannot be created on a piece of paper. She knew she was teaching the potential depth of the abstract visual stimulus."

"It has been thirty or forty years since many of us were in class with her," says Midori Imatake, a designer who practices in Japan, "but our appreciation for her process and philosophy has deepened, and I believe that the wisdom and validity of what she taught has been confirmed by what science has learned about the brain's visual function."

The 1960s spelled hard times for structured approaches to education. "Foundation flies in the face of the cafeteria/self-feeding approach," says Eugene Garfinkle, who taught at Pratt during that beleaguered time. Foundation became a rearguard activity. Many of Rowena's original colleagues had died or retired. She still had around her a small group of dedicated teachers from the early years, including Ivan Rigby and Robert Kolli (who had become chairman of the department after Kostellow's death) and others whom she had trained, Bill Fogler, Richard Welch, Gerry Gulotta among them. But fewer faculty than before taught full-time, and others came from schools and disciplines that did not honor what they saw as outdated or irrelevant methods. Although the task of preserving foundation looked like a losing battle, Rowena would not cede defeat."

Rowena Reed became head of Pratt's industrial design department in 1962. During the next four years, under her direction, students in the department prepared two important exhibitions of their work: one in 1965 at the IBM gallery in Manhattan and the other at Expo '67 in Montreal, where Pratt was one of three American design schools chosen to participate in the ICSID Designer's Pavilion. Deadlines, budgets, and students strained nearly beyond endurance didn't deter her from her inviolable practice, which was to scrutinize, criticize, and do it over and over until it was right. Sculptor Jon Pai, who studied with Rowena in the mid sixties, recalls, "I remember when we were preparing the exhibit at the IBM gallery. I walked into the space one day, and there were faculty just sitting there, looking glum. They weren't saying a word. Then I saw Rowena across

the room, standing by herself, her arms folded, holding her ground. She didn't like the color of the wall. She demanded that it be repainted, and she wouldn't let go."

By the time she retired from full-time teaching in 1966, the name Rowena Reed was synonymous with Pratt industrial design. "The Pratt approach was the Rowena Kostellow approach," Arthur Pulos wrote. "It was Rowena who brought the preoccupation—if that's the word for it—for plastic form to Pratt. She saw forms as being the one thing that the industrial designer can do that no one else can do."

"She became," Bill Fogler asserts, "the premier arbiter of form and space in industrial design."

Rowena Reed was named professor emeritus and continued to teach her space analysis course for twenty more years. She judged sculpture and design competitions, and lectured in schools and to professional organizations throughout the country and in Europe. She continued to act as an outspoken advocate for the industrial designer and for industrial design education.

"Industrial design started out as a reaction against the purely mechanical work that the engineers were doing," she declared. "There was a need for someone to design objects that make a definite design statement. Industrial designers were brought in to save industry, and they did. Industrial designers put industry on its feet in this country, and they've never gotten credit for it....Our government has never supported schools of design as they do in some European countries, and Europe supports design in other ways. Money spent on public relations creates a climate favorable to good design and makes the consumer more aware of it. This in turn makes the designer feel that his contribution is important. This country, which has benefited the most from design, has given the profession little recognition and support."

"She really was a missionary," sculptor Jon Pai says. "She had that missionary spirit—an idealization of how society could become transformed—and a belief that designers could do it."

The design statement she looked to industrial designers to make was a statement about the visual qualities of objects. "She didn't care where you put the motor," Bruce Hannah says. And Louis Nelson adds, "Her point of view about function was that you learned about it somewhere else."

In a speech delivered in Paris at the 1962 International Conference of Industrial Designers, she chastised those who would reduce design to the pursuit of structural or functional solutions. "They refuse to concede that visual organization may be a discipline in itself and necessary to the designer, or that the conceptual thinking of a design-oriented person can possibly approach that of the engineer." Rowena warned her students: "Never let function be an excuse for a bad design."

During the decade of the 1970s, she was awarded the Bronze Apple design award by the New York chapter of the Industrial Designers Society of America and the Design in the Americas award of the IDSA Congress in Mexico City. In 1972, Pratt awarded her its Distinguished Visiting Faculty Award.

Jerry Ross, Jerry Okuda, Charles Eames, Rowena Reed, and Joe Parriott

Semiretirement had its drawbacks. Rowena Reed was an intensely social person. She had never organized her life to allow much time alone. Now, as she entered her seventies, the apartment in Queens that she had lived in for thirty-five years seemed far from the center of things. In 1972, she gave it up and moved to an unfinished loft in SoHo.

The rehabilitation of the neighborhood between Houston and Canal Streets had just started, but artists and designers, including some of her former students, were beginning to move in, and Rowena felt the promise. "I think this will be an interesting place to live," she said and, against the judgment of family and friends, took possession of the big brick-walled loft overlooking West Houston Street.

She relished the large open space, separating living and working spaces with bookcases and placing her bed in the center of the loft. She designed a galley kitchen with storage below the counters, so she wouldn't have to reach up, and without an oven, because the only one beautiful enough to live with was far beyond her budget. (A former student bought her a toaster oven.) She brought along her Eames chairs, her grand piano, and Jacques, the Siamese cat. Her beloved Volvo stayed behind. She had Alexander's paintings hung high on the walls. Once a month, a local florist delivered an oversize bundle of laurel, which she stood in a large container near the door.

She became a familiar figure in the neighborhood. She was the fine-boned lady in cape and gaucho hat who bought gourmet food at Dean & DeLuca, had her red hair colored and coiffed at a salon on West Broadway and shopped with the ingenues at agnès b. "She loved good things, including couture clothes and fine food," remembers RitaSue Siegel, a student in the 1960s who is principal of a leading design search and consultancy firm. "She was really quite poor, living on a small retirement pension, but when exposed to the luxuries of life, she took them in stride as if she were used to them."

At the request of several former students, she began holding tutorials in the loft. The "Saturday class" attracted working designers and architects seeking the abstract experiences and rigorous critiques that only she provided. In her part-time teaching at Pratt, she focused on some new "experiences" she had begun to develop during her final years as a full-time teacher. These were the space analysis exercises. (Students called them "space boxes.") They were an extension of an early foundation problem in architectonics, an ambitious exploration of negative and positive space and the fulfillment of her deepest interest. "Personally, I respond to the whole concept of space so strongly," she said. "I've seen people who are very sensitive to form or organic volume but are practically blind when it comes to space. I want to make them

Pratt's exhibit in the ICSID show in the Designer's Pavilion at the Montreal Expo '67

more aware." She became engrossed in expanding her own understanding of spatial relationships and raising her students' level of sensitivity to them.

There are those, like ceramist Eva Zeisel, who taught with Reed in the early Pratt days, who believe that she was responsible for creating a "style" in design. "She influenced generations of students," Zeisel says, "and asymmetry

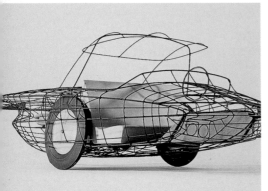

was one of her main ways of expressing her ideas. The fact that it had to be asymmetrical was a style. I don't know where it came from—this antagonism to classical organization—but through her teaching, it became the prevalent aspect of thousands of objects and buildings."

Gerry Gulotta believes it came from her own need to explore and discover. "Symmetry is a beautiful concept, but what is symmetrical is seen instantly," he explains. "There's no adventure, no investigation. For her, it was just never part of the deal."

Reed herself justified the focus on asymmetry in her teaching as a pedagogical strategy. "Symmetry can be beautiful, but symmetry is easy," she told her students. "Any dancer can stand straight on two feet. It's assuming a dynamic posture with one leg in the air that's difficult. We demand the dynamic axis because most people can't handle it. You strengthen your design muscles by becoming disciplined, by learning to do the most difficult things. That will allow you to express yourself more clearly and strongly because you will be able to control exactly what you want to say."

Lucia DeRespinis, a designer and teacher who studied with Reed and Kostellow in the early 1950s, explains: "Rowena did influence her students' designs by her enthusiasm for dynamic movement. She didn't get as excited about quiet, static design." But there's strong resistance to the idea that she fostered a style. "There was no more of a 'style' being taught in Miss Reed's class than in a strictly regimented ballet class," Gina Caspi insists. "The exercises are specific and pointed to strengthening weaknesses in given areas. But just as each dancer uses that discipline for his or her own expression, so has each of Miss Reed's students."

"Rowena maintained a focus on the process," explains environment and exhibit designer Ralph Appelbaum, "not on product. She didn't lead students to forms that dialog with style because she kept the focus on the eyes and on feelings."

She was less concerned with any particular formal solution than she was with the use of the cultivated intuition that made beautiful formal solutions possible. "She was intuitive and analytical," says George Schmidt, an industrial designer and teacher who studied with Rowena in the 1960s. "Her contribution was helping her students acquire an intuitive understanding of form and space. There aren't the same kind of rules there are in physics or math, but there are rules you can work by. It's a matter of understanding relationships, and that is more of an intuitive experience than a practical one."

"She understood that this is something that happens in a process," says Jon Pai. "You see it in master classes in music. Nothing you can write or talk about adequately captures that."

Rowena Reed influenced her students as much through her presence in the classroom as by her principles. She was quiet and imposing. She spoke softly and authoritatively in complete, precise sentences. She used physical gesture with conscious deliberation and to great advantage. (Once, looking at a snapshot of herself taken by a student, she exclaimed, "Notice how three-dimensionally I'm sitting!")

"She was an almost mythological figure—an icon," remembers jewelry designer Ted Muehling, "but she was also very direct and earnest and sincere. She had no irony, which made her a terrific influence in a time when everyone thought you had to be ironic to be intelligent."

She could be alternately subtle and disarming, and she had a relentless sense of purpose. A typical Rowena class consisted of a brief lecture followed by hours and hours of excruciatingly minute critique. "Frail, intense, and all business, she would perch on the corner of a desk and literally preach design," recalls Gene Grossman, founder and principal of Anspach Grossman Enterprise.

Then, one project at a time, she focused on her students' work. She would stare for a very long time, turning the exercise around and around, talking to what she saw from every angle. She'd comment on organization and balance, and, using a pointer, suggest trimming an eighth inch here or adding a sixteenth there. She demanded that all the students in the class focus on each individual's effort with her. She believed that students learned from others' successes and failures as well as their own. It was a singular experience for students to have someone look at their work that long and hard. Her powers of discrimination were uncanny. Her demands on students to create solution after solution for every problem could be exhausting. She'd stay until the last student exercise had been dissected.

"I still remember how she looked at a design," recalls Frank Grunwald, who studied with Rowena in the late fifties and is today manager of Global Design and Research at Thomson Consumer Electronics, "how closely she scrutinized it—from all angles, from close-up and from a distance—how her eyes analyzed each line, the movement of each plane. She was so intense. Nothing could distract her. She was always searching, looking for answers, trying to understand the form. Not just the surface of the form, but also the inner structure."

"There was something very pure about her communication," says Pamela Waters, a designer who studied with Rowena in the early sixties. "It wasn't about you. It was always about the work."

Not every student could endure the scrutiny, but the ones who did relished the experience. Debera Johnson, current chair of Pratt's industrial design department, recalls "twelve people trying to get as close as possible to Rowena's head to stare into these boxes. We'd be there for six hours doing it until, at the end of the day, we lost the light."

"Teaching for her was a ritual," Bill Katavolos explains. "She went into a crit so completely empty it was almost painful to watch. She had no preconceived notions whatsoever. She would just look at the work, turn it around, warm up, and go on for hours. I always admired that quality of going in with an open mind. It's the sign of a great teacher."

Richard Welch says, "Rowena had the greatest eye in the universe. You could go back after ten years, and she'd say, 'Yes...but this doesn't quite work.'" Her attention and standards of judgment were the same whether she was evaluating a senior project or a modern classic. "I forget who I'm talking to, and I talk to the design," she once explained.

"You could go to a museum opening of a deconstructivist show with her, and all the white-hot intellectuals would be there," recalls Bill Katavolos, "and Rowena would examine their work as if it were third year—student work.

Rowena Reed critiques a
student's spatial analysis
in the context of a useful-
purpose project

She'd be giving a crit—out loud—to an audience in white tie and tails that thinks it's at the leading edge of things, when it's at the tail end of what this woman had been doing for forty years."

The crit never ended. Bruce Hannah and Andrew Morrison, Rowena's students in the mid sixties, went on to design furniture for Knoll International. Hannah recalls the gala celebration marking the introduction of the Morrison/Hannah office chair. "Leading designers and architects were there, the press was there, and Rowena was there. A crowd gathered around as she talked about the design of the chair and showered us with compliments. The interview ended, the crowd dispersed, and Rowena slipped away. About a half hour later, I felt a tug on my sleeve. 'Bruce,' she said very softly, 'the rear curve of the arm is OK, but the front curve needs a little work.'"

She remembered her students' work better than they remembered their own. Years after the fact, she'd recall in detail one student's solution to the fragment problem or another's beautiful exercise in wire. (She could not, however, remember where she put her glasses or her keys, and almost every one of her acquaintances was, at one time or another, drawn into the search. Sometimes she misplaced bigger things. Students love to tell the story of the time she drove to Boston for a design conference and traveled home with a group on the train. She was back in Brooklyn for half a day before she remembered that her car was parked on a Boston street.)

She was completely engaged in her own time and lived always in the present tense. Even those who knew her for decades didn't know a lot about her childhood, her family, or her past in general. She did not reminisce. The few stories she told about her early life were stories that established the ground for the current experiences that absorbed her interest. She had a gift for friendship and nurtured long-term, personal relationships with many of her former students. They phoned at all hours, and came and went from her apartment, driving her to and from Pratt, taking her to lunch and dinner. They escorted her on her travels and slept on her couch when they came to town. They ran errands, helped her sort through piles of papers and slides, and brought her out to the country for weekends after she gave up her own country home.

She was a mentor to many students over the years, especially women. In the 1950s and 1960s, she encouraged female industrial design graduates to enter industries and companies—like General Motors—where few women had gone before. As the dominant figure in a mostly male discipline and profession, her encouragement bore the force of authority. Several of the women she mentored became serious disciples of her message. "She was teaching me not just for my own education but to make me a teacher, to help me carry the torch," Gina Caspi says. Caspi taught 3-D foundation with absolute fidelity to Rowena's language and method, and Kate Hixon assiduously preserves Rowena's language and curriculum in the courses in space analysis.

"She had the ability to act as a mentor to many people at the same time," says Ralph Appelbaum. "Usually a teacher has one student on whom they focus, but I know many people who left her class feeling that she was their mentor—perhaps without her ever realizing that she was. That's a very powerful thing for a teacher to have. She was a model for a way of being and thinking. Studying with her became a personal search."

Designer Louis Nelson observes, "Rowena had a way of making investments in things that were good. It isn't always easy in the real world to use the design principles, to have the time to explore them, but she influenced my management of design—the holding out to make something beautiful."

Rowena was committed to the teaching of visual principles through structured experiences and was convinced that you couldn't do your best work unless you had them. She never waivered in her absolute conviction that the experiences were essential to creating form. She liked to make the analogy with music: "Symphony musicians don't play by ear, and most artists are playing by ear. There can be a discipline of visual relationships that is comparable to the discipline of music, and it should be learned. Some students think, 'This will destroy my personality; this will take something away from me. I can't think when I feel.' But if you can't think and feel at the same time, you'd better not try to get an education at all."

And she was adamant that the only way to create three-dimensional form was to work three-dimensionally. It was her mantra. "All three-dimensional projects should be designed three-dimensionally. You can't develop a good three-dimensional design on paper. That's like drawing a piece of sculpture. You have to deal with negative space, and you can't do that in two dimensions."

She waged a lifelong war of words with the architecture profession over its two-dimensional approach to teaching and practice. "Are you drawing?" she demanded of a startled student in a space analysis class. Then, shaking her head as if to say I know what I'm going to hear, she asked, "What did you study before you came to this class?" When the student innocently allowed as how it was architecture, she counted to ten, slowly and out loud. "Well, that's the way the architectural profession works, and it's wrong," she finally announced. "You must learn how to think directly in three dimensions. If you know how to organize in space three-dimensionally, you can learn how to draw three-dimensionally, but it's not the way to design."

In fact, many of the students in the Saturday class were architects seeking to compensate for their lack of three-dimensional training. And at Pratt, George Schmidt recalls, "there were a number of students who came down to foundation from the graduate program and from architecture because they had heard about this person who talked about space like no one else did."

Her concepts for understanding visual abstraction—dominant, subdominant, and subordinate; tension; negative and positive space—were her codes for understanding the world. She applied them to every aspect of life, from judging character to negotiating the Brooklyn Bridge. Aiming her Volvo across three lanes of speeding traffic, she'd calmly explain to gasping passengers, "I'm the dominant driver."

She never hesitated to inform a student—any student—that they didn't understand what they were doing because they hadn't taken foundation. Pratt foundation. "It's like mathematics," she'd say. "I suppose you could start with calculus if you're really smart, but sometime someone's going to ask you to do a problem in long division. No matter how good you are, you'll be better with foundation than you would be without it."

Rowena would sometimes tell her students, "You don't feel this yet, but ten years from now, you'll hear my voice inside your head; and because you can finally see it, you'll understand it."

For Rowena, teaching was lifelong learning. "Teaching is a marvelous adventure—like having a huge laboratory in which to carry out experiments," she explained. "I was clarifying for myself what I felt was missing in my own education. I kept on teaching the same essential things, but I was digging deeper every year, trying to make it clearer to myself and to other people."

Rowena Reed suffered a heart attack in the fall of 1988. Just as she had been surrounded by family and friends throughout her life, she was surrounded by them in her final days. Near the end, as her eyesight failed, she mourned her inability to carry on her daily, ritual reading of the New York Times. She died on September 14, 1988.

She insisted always on the designer's primary role as form giver.

"Not enough time and attention are given to the designer's first responsibility: to find and develop the visual solutions for living in our environment," she declared. "Of course, a product is no good to anyone unless the function is properly worked out. The object should express what it is very directly, but it is possible for a design to express what it is and also be a beautiful object in its own right.

"We introduce the student to an ordered sequence of purely visual experiences by which an artist may develop his understanding and his recognition of the abstract elements in any design situation. Our goal is the training of a designer so familiar with the principles of abstraction that he automatically thinks of a visual problem in terms of organized relationships and then feels free to study other aspects of the problem or to confer with specialists in related fields. He is a designer who can visually cross boundaries and suggest new forms for new materials or new techniques."

— Rowena Reed Kostellow

Rowena Reed, photographed by Lou Sgroi for the cover of I.D. Magazine, **November/December 1982**

PART II
FOUNDATION

"There have been many theories of design

and many valuable ways of analyzing

both graphic and three-dimensional

situations, but the unique quality of this

curriculum which I am about to present

is that it is structured in a way which

quite literally covers any combination of

design relationships which you may

encounter and enables you to organize

the abstract relationships for yourself."

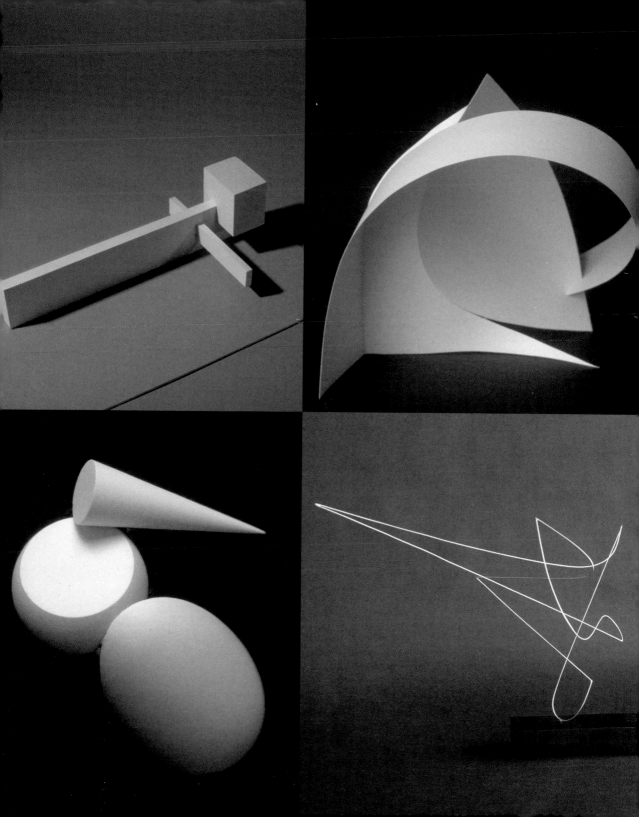

TO BEGINNING STUDENTS OF THREE-DIMENSIONAL DESIGN
OCTOBER 22, 1982

For those of you who have never worked in three dimensions, foundation provides an introduction to the three-dimensional world and to that complex and exciting set of relationships that will challenge you for the rest of your lives. There is no end to it. I would hope that some of you might pursue this search for its own sake, as the scientists do, pausing from time to time for a personal expression that could lead to new paths to explore.

For those of you who have had three-dimensional experiences, and have known the frustration of never completely understanding what you were doing (as I have) or have become stuck at a certain point in the development of a project, the experience of going back to the beginning and proceeding from simple to complex relationships will provide great satisfaction, a sense of freedom, and the security that comes from knowing that you can realize the potential of your idea because you can study it objectively.

The study of abstract relationships is not easy. It is a long, slow process with its own frustrations—like any discipline—but the rewards are great and the trip is exciting. So I hope I may have your cooperation and your patience as we explore the first problem, which looks so simple and yet is almost a complete course in itself. It is an organization of three rectilinear volumes, and the objective is to achieve a familiarity with simple volumes and a unified statement.

ON SKETCHING

Three-Dimensional Sketches: All of the experiences in the foundation sequence and in the more advanced exercises start with three-dimensional sketching. Use whatever materials are appropriate to the problem: clay, paper, cardboard, bristol board, wire, glue....Work quickly. Make as many sketches of the abstract relationships as you can. The abstract relationships express the relation of the parts to the whole apart from any concrete or material embodiment. They reflect the direct visual experience of the thing, how forms and spaces and movements "speak" to one another.

In 1985, Gina Caspi spent six months in Italy transforming one of her four-inch Saturday class fragment problems into a ten-foot, three-ton marble sculpture.

Let your sketches be uninhibited. Later on you'll put the saddle on them. The sketches are the most fun. That's when you can be as creative and adventurous as you like. I believe in small sketches. If they're small, you make

more of them, and you don't get stuck too soon. Having ten ideas is like having ten children. You're not likely to spoil one to death. So let your ideas flow. Let them come out. But let them come out three-dimensionally.

Stand back and react to what you've done. Always react to your design sketches first. You can analyze them later. Focus on the ideas that seem the most interesting and exciting. Following the directions for an exercise doesn't guarantee that you'll create a design statement, but once you've selected one or two sketches for further work, you can use the visual principles you've learned to analyze them, develop the ideas, and refine your design statements.

Proportion Sketches: You can gain additional insight into the proportions and balance of your design by doing some two-dimensional sketches. Using 18" x 24" newsprint sheets and standing about ten feet away, draw several views of your three-dimensional sketch. With the flat side of a charcoal or pastel and with broad strokes, draw the gesture of your design. Then draw the full shape of the outside configuration. Squint when you do this, and draw as if the composition were out of focus and you could see overall shape but no detail. The outside shape should have a balance of directional forces from all views. (The balance of directional forces is the sum of all forces of movement.) Draw the silhouette down to the base and up again if that's what you see. The overall proportions should be an abstraction. Don't draw exactly what you see. These proportion sketches are an opportunity to explore and improve what you have in your three-dimensional sketch.

Space Sketches: The space sketch is a three-dimensional exercise that lets you explore the grouping of forms and the awareness of negative volume. It is a way of getting the overall concept out without having to struggle with materials. Use your space sketch to establish the first big tensional relationship between planes and volumes, or between groups of planes and volumes. Make it no larger than twelve inches. This three-dimensional sketch must suggest the proportions of the total negative volume, establish a balance of directional forces for every position, and establish complementary relationships between forms. The tensional relationship depends on sensitivity to the negative space between forms. You'll find that volumes will need to be placed farther apart than planes. Look at the positive forms after you've established the spatial relationships. Organize volumes, planes and lines—in that order. The space around the planes or volumes must be stimulated by the positive forms. This is an exercise in learning how to think of all these things at the same time, so everything in your final design relates to everything else.

PROBLEM ONE: RECTILINEAR VOLUMES

"At first, working with three-dimensional

forms in this way is difficult, but soon you

will begin to speak this language.

You really have to make these beautiful.

That sounds pretentious. How can you

make three blocks beautiful?

…But I know that you can."

Make up to fifty rectilinear volumes in clay in a wide variety of shapes. Clay is the best medium because you can both add to and take away with relative ease. The edges should read as clearly as possible. Organize the rectangles in groups of three, keeping these principles in mind:

Appreciate the qualities of contrasting shapes. The volumes you choose should vary in character as much as possible, and no two should have the same measurements. Learn to assess the volume of an element by eye, without measuring.

Establish relationships between the volumes by choosing dominant, subdominant, and subordinate forms. The *dominant* volume is the largest element, the most interesting and dramatic in character. It occupies the dominant position in the group.

The *subdominant* complements the dominant in character. Unless there is a twenty percent improvement in the character of the dominant when the subdominant is added, more experimentation is needed. The dominant/subdominant relationship can be very exciting, due not only to contrasts in character but to position as well. More often than not, the relationship is enhanced if the axes are not parallel.

"The dominant/subdominant is a very important relationship. The first obligation of these forms is to be complementary. They have to be very good for each other—like ham and eggs."

The *subordinate* makes the design still more interesting by introducing a third visual element and axis. The subordinate should make the design more three-dimensional, complement the existing forms, and complete the unity of the design. It is not as independent as the dominant or subdominant. It should be contrasting but sensitive to the other forms. It must be designed to fill what is missing in the other two.

Be aware of proportions: overall, inherent, and comparative. The *inherent* proportion refers to the proportions within a form: length to width to thickness.

The *comparative* proportions are the proportions of one form in relation to another. Think of a tall, thin person compared with a short, stocky one.

The *overall* proportion refers to the character or overall configuration of a group of forms. (If you squint and look at the silhouetted proportions of a group of forms, you're seeing its overall proportions.) No view should be uninteresting in character. In general, in these experiences, you should exaggerate the vertical in some and the horizontal in others. Most students make a horizontal overall proportion—perhaps because it seems more stable. Never emphasize the cube.

"Like a piano teacher, she
made you do the exercises
over and over so many
times that you lost all
your tricks."

— *Tucker Viemeister*

Subordinate——

Dominant——

Subdominant——

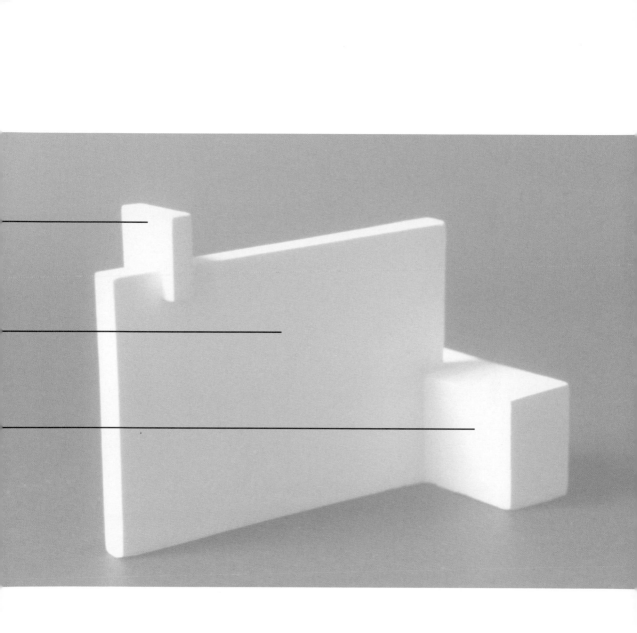

It's important to vary the proportions in your design. Make it interesting. The last thing you want is a predictable sequence of forms that looks like "going-going-gone."

The difference between beautiful and ordinary form is the sensitivity of these proportions. It is an intangible but very real quality. Understanding it is one of the most valuable assets of a visual artist. Too much time cannot be spent in developing this sensitivity in oneself and becoming intuitively aware of beautiful relationships.

Carefully position the axes of the volumes. The *axis* refers to an imaginary line through the center of the longest dimension of the form and indicates the strongest movement of the form. The axis gives a form its position in space. In all of the problems, we try to give each volume its own position in space.

In this exercise, keep the axes of the volumes static (perpendicular to each other). The *static axis* is the simplest and will help you get away from flat compositions. Later, in more advanced exercises, you will try to achieve a variety of movements of the axes. In fact, to make your designs more three-dimensional, you should use as many movements of the axes as possible. But for now, we start with a simpler challenge.

Always conceive a design from all positions. Work on a sturdy turntable, and continually rotate the sketch to make sure it "reads" from all directions.

Consider how the volumes are joined. There are three ways to join the voumes: *piercing, wedging,* and *cradling.*

Ask yourself the following questions as you look at your design:

Is there contrast between the dominant and subdominant forms?

Are they complementary? Are they too similar in size and shape? Students sometimes have a tendency to repeat the same dimensions.

Is the dominant form in the most prominent position? Students like to put the dominant form on the bottom because that seems to hold things up, but it's not necessarily the dominant position.

Does the subordinate form add something to the three-dimensional quality and unity of the whole? Sometimes there's a tendency to treat the subordinate as an orphan.

Does the design look good from all sides, at eye level, and from the top?

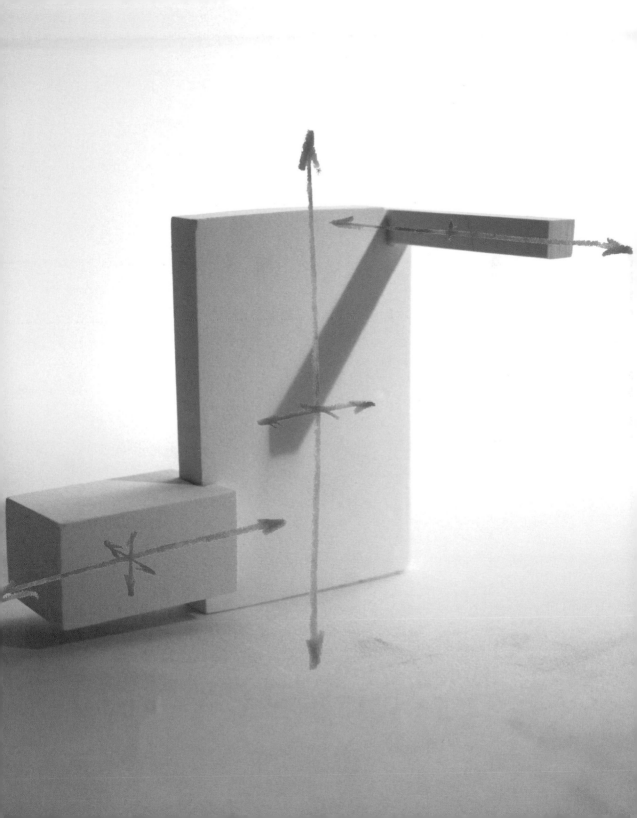

The challenge here is to create a unity from forms as essentially different in character as possible. Start by designing the dominant, then the subdominant. Spend a little time on this relationship. Quickly complete the subordinate element, and arrange in as three-dimensional a grouping as possible. This will give you a sense of the overall configuration. Then you can begin to refine. Emphasize either the vertical or horizontal proportion in each sketch. All joinings should appear structural. A balance of directional forces should be established. The design should look interesting and three-dimensional from every position. It should achieve an effect of unity in which every part relates to every other part, and every design relationship contributes to the whole.

"Think of the balance of your design as if you were a dancer. If the the axes of your arms and legs don't support the axes of your neck and torso, you'll fall over."

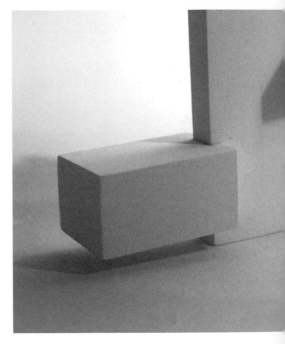

Unity is the visual glue that holds everything together. You know that you have achieved it when all the visual relationships within the design are organized in such an exquisite dependent relationship that every element supports and strengthens every other and any minor change would upset the perfect balance and tension.

Take your best sketch and develop it in plaster. You may want to make your plaster sketch larger than your clay piece—perhaps one and a half or two times larger. Differences in proportion will become more apparent as you enlarge the design.

Enlarging isn't simply a matter of copying. It requires you to pay attention to subtle changes in order to achieve a harmonious whole.

Be sure to use Hydrocal. The mixture is harder and comes out cleaner than standard plaster.

Wedging

"It's important not to mix apples and oranges. Every one of the problems is meant to develop and clarify a very particular visual issue. If you overlap, then you mix them up. Miss Reed was very specific about that. If the only thing a student learns from the first problem is that one thing can make another look good by being near it, they've learned something very valuable."

— *Gina Caspi*

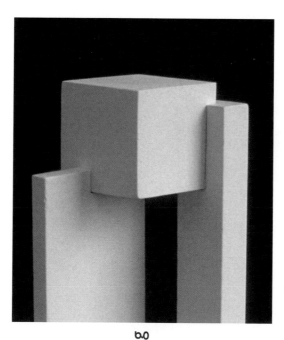

Cradling

Piercing

PROBLEM TWO: CURVILINEAR VOLUMES

"Now you will build on your experience

with rectilinear volumes in a static

composition by taking on a more

complicated challenge. The second

experience involves the organization of

curvilinear volumes in a dynamic

relationship. In addition to mass,

proportion, and character, you will now

deal with the additional challenge of

the diagonal axis. We will work with

curvilinear solids.

   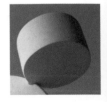

sphere

hemisphere

cone

cylinder

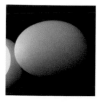

ovoid

ovoid plinth

half ovoid

round plinth

Start by making many curvilinear volumes in clay. Make volumes of varying proportions to explore their properties. The jump from rectilinear to curvilinear is a big one because the new shapes are harder to handle. Create a dynamic composition by combining any three curvilinear volumes. Keep the following principles in mind:

Choose forms that are pleasing in and of themselves. Then consider the complementary relations of mass, proportion, and character. (Everybody seems to love cones, so I'll tell you something about them that will help your design. A slender cone is easier to see as dominant or more interesting than a fat cone. You can structure slender cones so they don't fall over by cutting a piece from a wire hanger, filing a point, dipping in white primer, and inserting it into the cone.)

Position the axes. This problem is primarily a design of the axes to make your sketch three dimensional and interesting from all directions. Use the diagonal axes to create movement in space. You don't want your composition to look like three forms stuck together. The volumes should be in dynamic relationship. There should be tension—a vibrating relationship—between the axes of the volumes. *Tension* is the point of increased awareness between the axes of volumes, planes, or lines. (It can also relate to color, value, and texture.)

Establish dominant, subdominant, and subordinate relationships. The largest volume doesn't have to be on the bottom. You don't want to build like bricks. The top is more likely to look like the dominant position. Put the most interesting shape in the dominant position. A form has to be doubly dramatic in character if it's going to be on the bottom. Preserve the identity of the individual forms while creating a composition that is larger, more dramatic, and more interesting than any single volume standing alone.

Be sensitive to proportions: inherent, comparative, and overall.

Consider the way elements are joined. The joints are part of the design. It's not usually successful to have one form piercing another unless the one doing the piercing is slender.

Make a statement about how the composition is to be perceived. Don't give choices. Force the eye to take in all three forms and to move through your design in a specific way.

Be aware of the volume of air within which your design exists. Try to activate the negative volume around and between your positive forms.

Create a balance of directional forces from every position if possible. The composition shouldn't look flat from any vantage point. No one view should look more than twenty percent more interesting than another view. The two largest forms in your design should accomplish more than two-thirds of the balance. The balance of directional forces is the sum total of the forces of movement within a composition. One

"These exercises are running the scales. You have to be able to strike the notes before you can play the music."

— *James Fulton*

adds it up subconsciously. Either it feels right or it doesn't. A sensitivity for balance can be acquired over time. It develops with practice and experience.

Think of dependent and independent visual balance. Each form in your composition should be responsive to every other form. Strive to create a total experience in which all of the elements work together.

Dependent balance describes a situation in which the axis of a volume, plane, or line needs the axis (axes) of other volumes, planes, or lines for physical structure or to feel structural to the eye. It also applies to a group movement in which three or four forms are dependent on one another for balance, and to one group movement in relation to another (that is, when the gesture of one group needs the gesture of an opposing group to achieve balance).

Independent balance refers to the condition in which a line or volume in a static composition is independently related to the vertical or the horizontal axis. Curved lines or volumes in composition are independently balanced when each appears to be in the best possible position for itself regardless of whether or not it is physically supported by other curves or straight lines.

Precarious balance describes the situation in which one gets the feeling of balance but ever so slightly—as when a dancer is suspended for a moment in space or on toe. It is as though, for a split second in time, the gesture is holding its breath. The very thrust of the gesture seems to support itself for the moment.

Work on developing a sense of visual structure. Think of the position(s) in which a form, standing alone, is comfortable. For example, does a given cylindrical volume look more or less comfortable in a resting position (horizontal or vertical) or at a forty-five degree angle? How far over can it lean and still appear comfortable? The total composition should look structural. It should appear to be self-supporting. It should look like a physical structure as well as a design structure.

It's all design organization. All the directions regarding proportion in the first problem apply here. In addition, here we have three kinds of tension. First, tension between the axes of the volumes. They have to be very sensitive to each other. Second, tension between the surfaces of the planes. They must be aware of each other. (Actually, tension is just an increased awareness.) And third, tension between the accents of the curves (that is, the areas of greatest expansion). You must try to find the most interesting tensions you can because that will change the positions—and for the better.

Always ask yourself, "Is this an interesting design idea? Does it make a design statement?" The process of doing these problems is like reflexology—like pressing a spot on the foot. The way you know you're pushing the right spot is that it hurts.

"She taught us a visual three-dimensional language, and the intrinsic organization and structure of her teaching was akin to the teaching of a written language. There were rules like the rules governing the structure of a sentence. The structure isn't in or out of fashion—it just is."

— *Robert Anders*

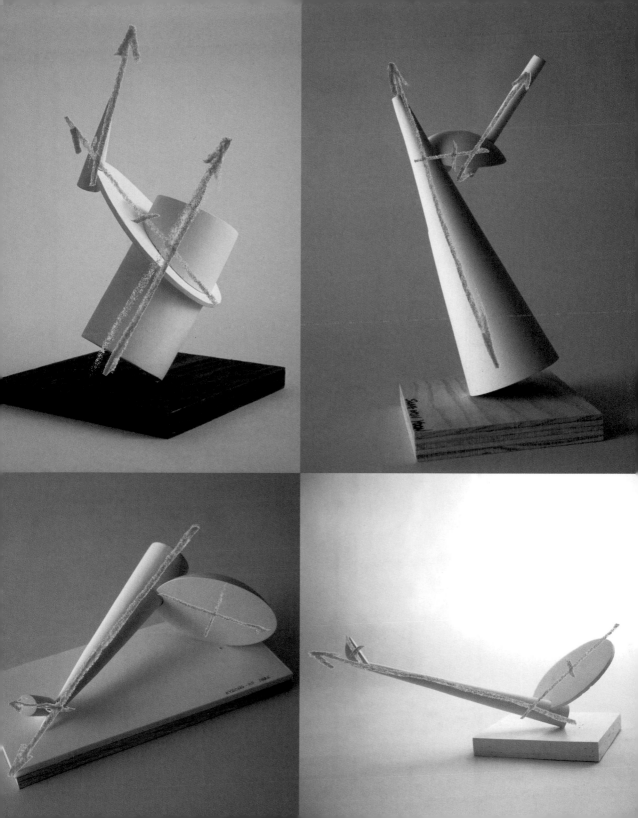

PROBLEM THREE: RECTILINEAR AND CURVILINEAR VOLUMES

"The beauty of this process is that you may not apply these principles directly when you're doing a project like a car interior or a lamp. But you bring to that process a sensitivity to composition that helps you make the right choices."

— *Gerald Gulotta*

"In this problem we introduce the

notion of group movements."

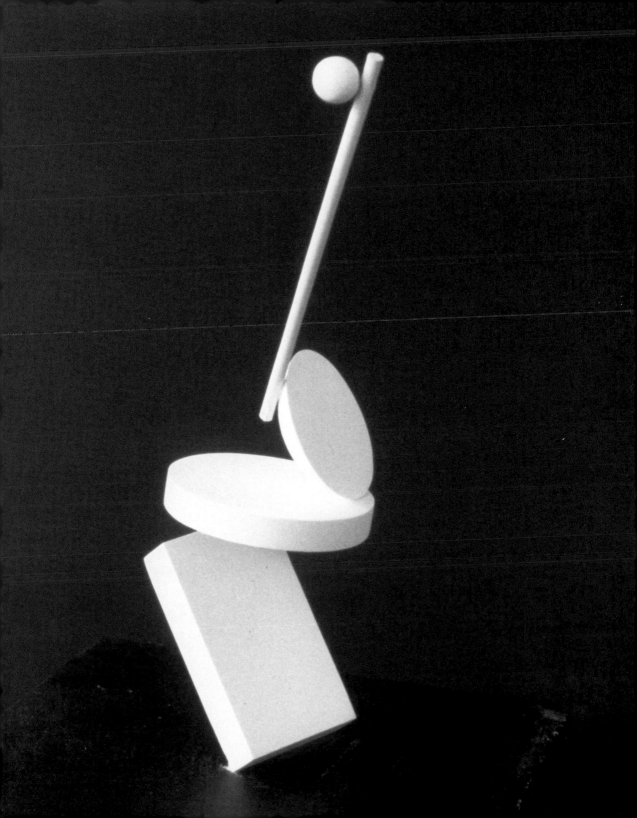

Make a variety of rectilinear and curvilinear volumes in clay. Combine five to seven rectilinear and curvilinear forms of your choosing in a relationship that has dynamic balance. Apply the principles you learned in the first two exercises.

Establish dominant, subdominant, and subordinate relationships. Be aware of inherent, comparative, and overall proportions.

Every form in your composition must have its own individual position in space, but it must work together in rhythm with the others. The most important consideration here is the balance of directional forces.

"It's good to remember your first emotional response."

Establish visual continuity by positioning the axes. Be aware that dominant, subdominant, and subordinate refer to the movements of the axes as well as to the masses and volumes of the forms. The forms can physically touch, but they should be visually separate. Don't make a long string of things. Create a composition in which you feel one movement stop and another complement it.

The sum of all the forces and movements in your composition should "add up." Look at your work from all points of view. Don't just look at the good view. Look at the bad view, and make what's not working work.

PROBLEM FOUR: FRAGMENTS

"The objective of this exercise is to choose

a solid, cut it apart, and reorganize the

cut fragments in a new composition that

is more beautiful than the original form

from which it was derived."

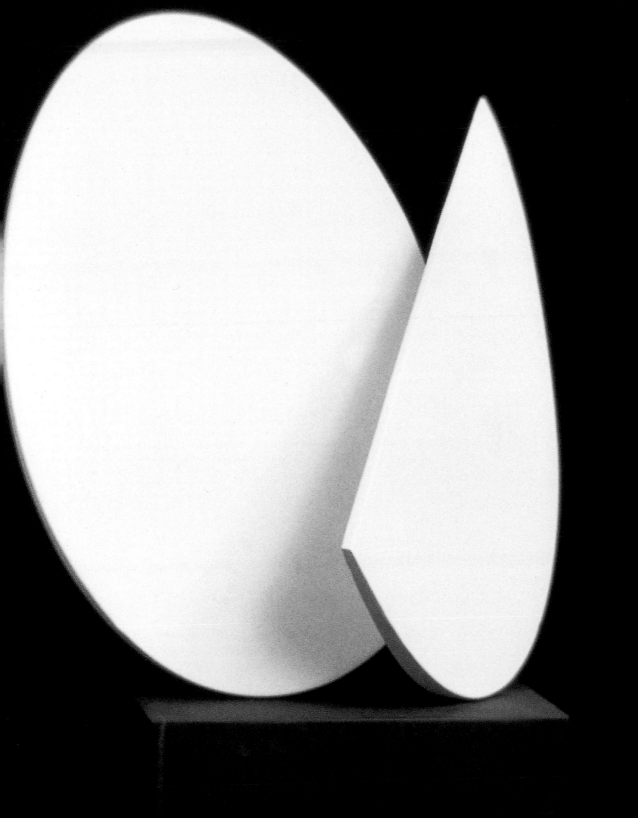

This is the first time in the foundation curriculum that you are asked to create your own form. You can work with any of the following simple geometric solids: sphere, hemishpere, cylinder, cone, ovoid, ovoid plinth, round plinth, rectilinear solids (of which there are many).

Design one or two geometric solids. Start by making four to six sketches in clay and choosing the ones you like best. You will find that it's easiest to work with heavy, compact geometric shapes. Design forms that are interesting and beautiful in proportion. The forms should differ in size and character. If you choose to work with two solids— for example, a rectilinear solid and a cone of contrasting proportion—you may fragment both, or fragment just one and use the other whole.

Divide the solid into at least three fragments. Use a clay knife to make straight cuts and twenty-four-gauge copper wire to cut curves. You'll find that it's not difficult to cut two interesting fragments, but it's very difficult to get a third fragment that doesn't look like a leftover. You must ask yourself, What does each cut do to the part that remains? The consequences of your actions become immediately apparent. Don't be too ingenious with your cuts, and don't feel compelled to destroy the geometric quality of the form.

If, after cutting a fragment, you decide to make that part smaller, you must return the clay to the piece from which it was cut, making that piece larger. In other words, if you take something, you have to give something back. If a part is missing in the final composition, you will intuitively sense its absence.

Group the forms to create a beautiful composition. Use toothpicks or straight pins to hold your design together. You must use all of the fragments from the original solid, and they must add up—physically and visually—to a harmonious whole.

"In my experience, all designers have particular areas of sensitivity. But sensitivities can be developed. Flounder around for a while. A dancer can't say, 'My back isn't very strong, so I won't use my back.' The beauty of this course is that if you do all the exercises in the proper order, you will find the weak points in your intuitive responses and will strengthen them so that you will become a better, all-round designer."

Establish dominant, subdominant, and subordinate relationships. Apply the same criteria to the fragment problem that you did to the simpler problems that deal with whole shapes. If one shape overwhelms another, it's not really a dominant-subdominant relationship. The fragments must complement each other. Every element should help the other elements look better. Make some proportion sketches to experiment with creating a sense of visual unity.

This exercise gives you experience in working with positive forms and negative volume at the same time. Be aware of the negative volume in your composition. Create tensional relationships between the positive forms and between the positive forms and the negative volume.

Make a unified visual statement. You want to achieve a unified visual statement right from the beginning. The fragment problem can end up looking like a lot of scraps piled together—or it can be a design with real character. The success of the solution depends a great deal on the grouping of forms.

Be careful not to take forms that are interesting in themselves and place them in an obvious arrangement with other forms (one-two, one-two, one-two). And be aware that if one part of your composition is very complex while another part is very simple, the design probably won't unify. Your composition should look completely different from the original form but should be as balanced and even more beautiful.

Be aware of the movement of the axes. Think of that movement when you position each fragment. If you have all your fragments except one in dynamic positions, that lonely little static fragment will be difficult to unify with the whole.

You may want to use small sticks to make some axis sketches as experiments in creating structure and balance. Create an abstraction of as many lines or groups of lines as possible, making them go in and out of space. This will help you gain an understanding of movement within a complex group of forms. If concavities are created, the lines of the concavity should move three-dimensionally. There's a tendency for students who haven't worked three-dimensionally with lines to make them flat. (There's a catch here. It's helpful to be able to analyze all of the lines of the concavities created in the fragment problem by using the method developed in the wire problem. But I don't assign the wire problem before the fragment problem because I believe that the fragment should be more geometric in character. Otherwise it becomes more sculptural and too complex for students to grasp, and much is lost.)

IN GENERAL...

Spend fifty percent of your time designing a geometric solid that is interesting and beautiful, and the rest of the time working with the fragments. If the proportions of the original are beautiful to start with you have a better chance of getting beautiful fragments from it. You must love the proportions that you've made. If you choose to work with two solids, take time and care to create forms that complement each other before you begin fragmenting them.

Keep all of your three-dimensional sketches. Don't destroy your early attempts as you create more successful compositions. You will find it very helpful to compare them.

"She would put things on the floor and look down—and that was a revelation. Most of us worked from a fixed position. Rowena taught us to get five to twenty feet away and see our work in its entirety, look at it from all sides and from the top down, to see it in a different way from the way we worked on it. That was a very important lesson."
— *Len Bacich*

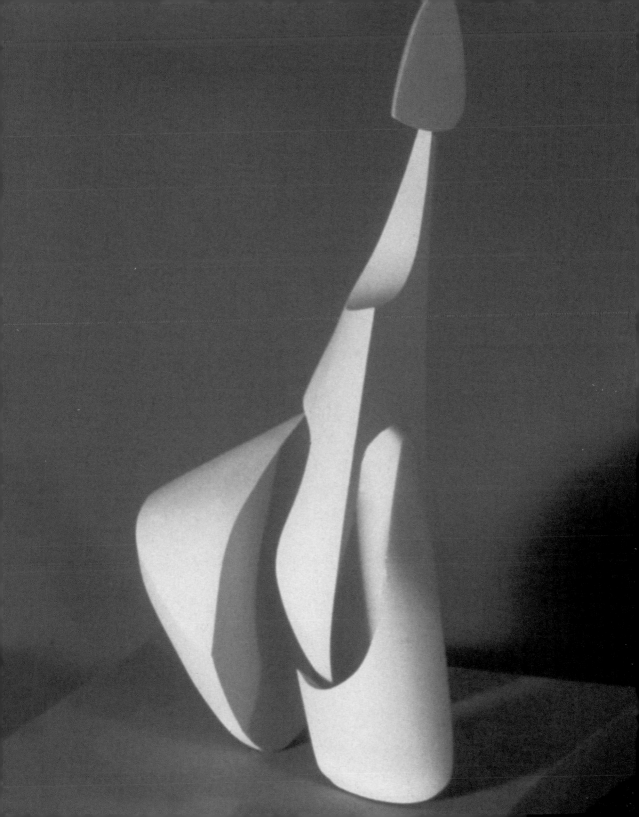

PROBLEM FIVE:
PLANAR CONSTRUCTION

"The objective of this exercise is to gain an

understanding of the characteristics of

planes and how they relate to each other

in space. In this problem, you are asked

to create a beautiful construction using a

variety of planes."

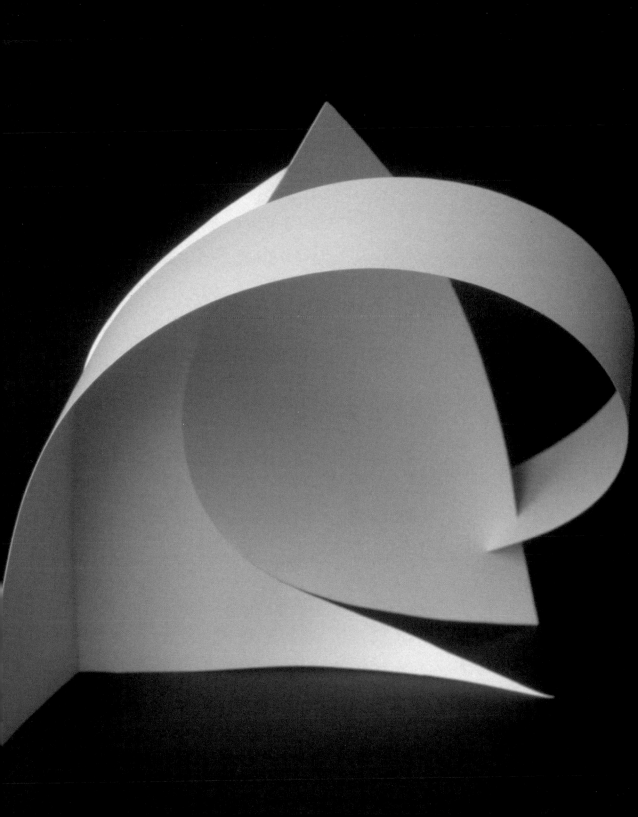

A plane is an element that has surface direction and slant unaccompanied by mass.

THERE ARE TWO- AND THREE-DIMENSIONAL PLANES:
Two-dimensional (flat) planes are characterized by their axes.

In *straight axis* planes, the axis moves in a straight line across the plane. The edges of the plane express the direction of the axis.

In *bent axis* planes, the axis moves across the surface of the plane in one direction and then shifts direction. The plane is flat, but the axis is bent.

In *curved axis* planes, the edges are curved, causing the axis to curve. The plane remains two-dimensional.

In *complex axis* planes, the axis changes direction (there are infinite possibilities), but no matter how complex its route, the outer edges of the plane visually "add up" to the course of the movements of the plane.

In general, the edges of a plane should express the axis. If the intention is to maximize the power of plane, the eye must move across the surface of the plane, not around its outside edge. Visual continuity across space is based on the way the surfaces slant. The edges of planes should never be shapes (movements) in themselves. They must relate to the whole.

"Don't work with the outlines first—ever, ever, ever!"

When one edge of a plane is cut, it affects all the other edges, thus influencing the movement of the axis. Our challenge is to see how well we can control the visual experience.

THREE-DIMENSIONAL PLANES ARE OF FOUR TYPES:
In a *curved plane,* the surface curves into more than one plane but doesn't twist through the transition. It is a simple curved surface.

In a *broken plane,* the plane bends in space at a hard edge through the transition.

In a *twisted plane,* as the plane moves in space, it twists, shifting the axis on its surface.

In *grouped planes,* three or more planes create a group movement or gesture. (Flat planes can also form a group.)

Begin by making a series of two- and three-dimensional planes. For sketching, use card-

two-dimensional planes

 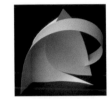  

straight axis

bent axis

curved axis

complex axis

curved plane

broken plane

twisted plane

grouped planes

board, bristol board, construction paper, oak tag, tape, stapler, glue gun and pellets, and wire (if needed for support). Experiment with proportion and character to experience the infinite potential of these forms. In all cases, the edges must visually express the desired axis and the quality of the plane.

Note: When cutting the outside edges of planes to make them curve in space, don't draw curved lines on paper to represent a desired curve. Forget about the outline. Start with a basically rectilinear surface, and curve it to the desired shape in your hands. Just make a beautiful gesture. Hold in position, and pencil in the changes. Cut a little at a time.

Next, do some three-dimensional sketches of ideas for interesting forms that might be created by planes shifting direction and slanting in space. Work with a combination of straight, bent, curved, broken, and twisted planes. You can tape them, glue them, notch them, attach them with tiny wires, and leave some standing alone. Experiment with vertical and horizontal orientation. Develop relationships between planes across negative space.

Here you are creating the design statement that will keep you on course as you develop your construction. If you don't have a strong design statement at the beginning, the analysis, rather than your visual intent, overtakes the idea. This is the passionate phase. Do it quickly, spontaneously, faster than your conscious mind can censor. Afterwards, we'll look at the ideas and refine them.

This is a very difficult problem, but it gives you a chance to express something that is visually your own. It will draw on your talent and creativity. Be patient. It may take you many hours to create an assemblage of planes that looks like something more than a pile of paper. Persevere until you have some examples that express a life force, a clear statement.

At this point, you may want to do some proportion sketches to evaluate and adjust your overall design idea.

Now you're ready to develop and refine your design statement. Focus on establishing two or three group movements. Try to activate the negative space between and around groups of planes. Establish tensional relationships between groups of planes. Your planar construction should express:

complementary contrast in types of planes

complementary contrast in proportion

harmony between the edges of planes and their axes: the edges should reflect the movement of the planes.

dependent balance: The positions of individual planes and groups of planes should "add up" to create a sense of visual balance from all directions.

space as position: Each plane should have a distinct direction in space. The number of positions should equal the number of individual planes.

space as opposition: When planes have discontinuous axes (i.e., the axis of one does not lead to the axis of another), visual continuity across space is achieved by the way the surface slants "add up."

group movement: The direction, axis, and slant (tipping of the surface) of a plane are continued by a change in the axis and slant of another plane. The visual character of the transition is determined by the angle of the line of intersection between the two planes. The intersection should happen at a place that feels natural in space. It should not feel like an arbitrary bend.

Before executing your planar construction in final materials, make a space sketch. For this experience, we do the sketch by making an outline of a box using sticks and glue. Make your open box in a proportion that best fits your design statement. Now make a shorthand version of your design within the box, using just a few planes and including the major movements. Study the space in and around your planar construction. Note that as the planes are slanted and tipped in space, the shifts affect the space. They can either kill it or make it come alive.

Once you have achieved a sketch in which proportions, position, movements, and the edges of the planes are pleasing, construct the design in final form using three-ply bristol board or museum board (two- or three-ply) and optional metal or styrene.

"Rowena taught me how to see. Nobody's ever taught me anything else as important as that."
— *Pamela Waters*

"She reminded me of a scientist. She was talking about abstract relationships almost the way a scientist would talk about electrons and protons, strong forces and weak forces."
— *William Katavolos*

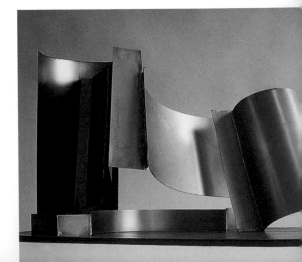

PROBLEM SIX:
LINES IN SPACE

"Lines have many uses in design. They

can be used as the axes of solid forms, to

describe planes or volumes, and to

delineate."

In our study of lines, we work with eleven curves and the straight line. They constitute our basic vocabulary of lines. The eleven curves are the typical curves used in design. Like the colors in a color chart, there may be many others in between, but they are similar curves with different proportions.

"Have a mental image of what you'd like the gesture to do, and that will dictate the proportions."

The curves we work with are neutral, resting, supporting, trajectory, hyperbolic, parabolic, reverse, catenary, directional, accented, and spiral.

THE FIRST THREE CURVES ARE SLOW CURVES:
The *neutral curve* is the most innocuous curve and perhaps the least dramatic. It's a segment of a circle. The accent is the same any place you look at it. It expands the same amount all along its length. (Recall that the accent of a curve is its point of greatest expansion.)

The *resting curve* stands in a balanced position on its accent, as if resting lightly on a molecule. It should not flatten out.

The *supporting curve* is just the opposite of the resting curve. If you put something on top of this curve—on the accent—it should feel like it is supporting the load, like a bridge.

THE NEXT FOUR ARE FASTER CURVES:
The *trajectory curve* is like the path of a ball being thrown or a hose emitting a stream of water. It starts straight and very fast, then falls off as the speed diminishes.

The *hyperbolic curve* appears to be similar to the trajectory but is actually quite different in character. It starts out straight and fast, but instead of slowly diminishing, it turns back toward the source, and its energy is concentrated in one spot.

The *parabolic curve* is not the mathematical equivalent of a parabola, but it does resemble one. It's a combination of the trajectory and the hyperbolic: its accent is not as strong as the former nor as open as the latter. It is a good curve to use in large-volume, organic forms. When we first began discussing these lines, we called it the General Motors curve because, in those days, all fenders looked like that. Actually, it shouldn't be symmetrical. That is, it shouldn't expand equally like a sphere but should have a little accent.

The *reverse curve* is one of the most interesting. It resembles the letter s but should have some verve, motion, and style. It's even more interesting when it has a little diagonal movement.

"Baryshnikov could jump ten feet in the air because he did his exercises. Rowena thought that way. You could do design because you did all the exercises. If you didn't know how to do the exercises, you couldn't do the work."
— *Bruce Hannah*

slow curves   fast curves

neutral

resting

supporting

trajectory

hyperbolic

parabolic   reverse   catenary   directional   accented   spiral

THE NEXT THREE ARE DIRECTIONAL CURVES:

The *catenary curve* is really a gravity curve. It is best demonstrated by a chain. If you hold one end of a chain in each hand, the accent is at the lowest point. Move your hands together, you'll get more of an accent; move them apart, and you'll get less. And you can move the accent from left to right by lowering one hand or the other.

The *directional curve* points like an arrow. One could say that it's not a curve at all, but a broken line. It has a very strong directional force.

The *accented curve* is similar to the catenary and directional curves, but it is slightly curved at the sides while the others have straight sides.

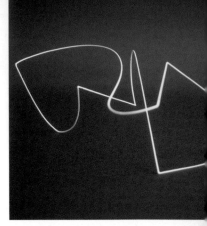

THE LAST CURVE IS "INDEPENDENT":

The *spiral curve* is hard to combine with other curves. It's a prima donna. It has so many possible accents, depending on the number of spirals within it, that you can't define them or create tensions between them. If wound loosely, for example, it looks like a snail. If wound very tightly, it's almost like a straight line.

Practice making a variety of curves. To get a feeling for these curves, you can begin by drawing them. Use news sheets and soft charcoal. Work loosely and as fast as you can, drawing many of each in different proportions. When you get the feel of each of the individual types, you are ready to make them in wire.

You'll need twenty-four-gauge copper wire and needle-nose pliers. The copper wire has a good tensional quality, especially after it's been stretched. Pull a length of wire from the spool using the pliers. Holding the end of the wire with the pliers and the wire at the spool with your hand, pull until the wire is tight. Hold for a moment, pull again to stretch the wire, then cut off the stretched piece.

Make your curves in the air. You can see them much better that way. Take your best examples, and mount them on a 24" x 36" board. This chart is your alphabet of curves, and you can refer to it as you work on the exercise "Lines in Space."

The purpose of this problem is to learn how to move lines in and out of space to the maximum. Move in and out as much as possible in the most three-dimensional way. In order to help you do that, I've worked out a formula that forces you to use a variety of curves and some straight lines that contrast with the curves to make the problem more interesting.

Choose four different curves and two straight lines. Of course, many other combinations are possible, but this is a good formula for a first experience. Use contrasting and complementary curves. Divide your lines into two groups (I would suggest you make groups of

> "Rowena told us, 'You should take the wire problem as your daily tonic.'"
>
> — Kate Hixon

> "All of a sudden, you dance with the line, and you know just what to do."
>
> — Gina Caspi

three). You will mount the two groups on a base and connect the two by soldering to form a single design.

Use wood bases (about a half inch thick), not foam core. You will need the weight of the wood to support the wire. Make a hole with an awl, and stick a piece of copper wire into the wood. The wire in your design will solder readily to it, and the connection will be almost invisible. Try to keep all your soldering joints very small.

Start with a piece of stretched wire about eighteen inches long. You're going to make three curves with this piece of wire. Don't start at the bottom and go up. Begin at the top, but do your design in relation to the base. Keep in mind what the bottom will be, and trust your intuitive sense of structure to guide you, so that when you mount the wire on the board, it looks like it will stand up. Don't start with a neutral curve because that's not exciting enough. Start with one with character, like a reverse curve.

Design your curve. Don't just bend it. Make a curve that uses the tension of the wire. Don't torture the wire too much. Each curve should stay in one plane. As it is, with six curves, you'll have six directions.

Decide which position your curve will look best in—where it will have the most character and be most lively. Decide on the plane, either at right angles to the base or tipped. If you're working with a fast curve, remember that if you keep it at right angles, you'll have a fast curve in a static position, which is almost a contradiction in terms.

When you've made your first curve and you're ready to make a turn into your next one, hold on to your first curve for dear life, and don't bend your wire by pushing it around. Just make a little angle with your pliers, hold very lightly, and move in another direction. You don't need to achieve complete balance in this first group of three because you still have the second group to work with.

Make your design dramatic. You might go from a reverse curve to a straight line because that's a good contrast. It's important to decide how long to make the line. Then move in the opposite direction, and make the third curve—perhaps an accented curve—or another curve of your choice.

Solder this first design to your base, making it look like the wire is resting on the wood.

"There was a Saul Steinberg exhibition in New York, and Rowena insisted that the class go. At the gallery, we watched her: this wirelike lady, with her wire kit dangling out of her handbag, looking at the wire like drawings. It was a great moment."

— *Ronald Beckman*

Now make your second group of three. Design the largest curve in your second group to complement the largest curve in the first group, and position them with as much distance between them as possible.

Create a tensional relationship between the accents of the two largest curves. It will take you a while to become sensitive to the tensions between curves, but persist. In time, you will achieve an instant recognition of the balance of all forces of movement, of all accents.

The second group of three curves, when combined with the first, should create a balance of directional forces from all directions. Keep turning the exercise around as you work to see it from all angles, and be sure to look at it from the top! Solder the ends of the first and second groups together only when you are satisfied with the design of the second group.

Remember that your objective in this problem is to find the most three-dimensional solution. Your lines should not delineate a volume. It's a common tendency, but it's not appropriate in this exercise. Your lines should look like they move separately in and out of space. Try to achieve lines that have the force of the curve. They have to move fast enough to support their positions. Avoid lines that look like they're made of wet string.

Beware of a *tweak*, in which the end of one curve is the same as the end of the next (like a leaf). It may be decorative, but it's not nice here; and in this problem, there's nowhere to hide. All the curves are out there and exposed.

Try to stay spontaneous. You can't do this problem cold bloodedly. The other problems may be approached in a more formal way, but this one can't be. You have to feel your way. It takes a lot of emotional energy, so you might want to do one or two of these exercises every night instead of doing many all at once.

This problem is like approaching infinity. You never get there. But the more you try the more uses you'll find for lines. This problem can be irritating because it looks easy and it's not.

If used properly, the wire problem can help you with any three-dimensional organization. However, it must be understood so well that you do not have to think very much. It can then be used quickly, creatively, and emotionally to make proportion sketches, visualize the design of axes and grouping of axes, suggest movement of planes, distort proportions meaningfully, and, in general, establish a very three-dimensional image.

"The wire problem was a musical model of Rowena's classes. If you could do the wire problem really well, you were like a jazz musician who could improvise. You begin with the theme, then you take it outside and walk with it, do transitions. But when you're done, it has to all hang together. Every piece has to complement what went before and what comes after."

—— Jeff Kapec

PART III
ADVANCED
STUDIES IN FORM

"Whereas in foundation the elements of

line, plane, volume, and space are

studied thoroughly in simple situations

with a high degree of control, the

advanced problems pose more complex

exercises, which involve the

interrelationships of these elements."

PROBLEM ONE: CONSTRUCTION

"The abstract experience based on

construction involves the design and

organization of contrasting forms, the new

experience of grouping forms to create

related movements, and a deeper

understanding of the balance of

directional forces and of tensional

positions in space."

The construction is made up of elements in a variety of materials, which may be used as found, or bent or shaped in some way, and then combined. Materials suitable for your construction include metals, plastic, glass (opaque or translucent), wire, string, rods, sheet metals, wood, stone, plaster, fiberglass, masonite, other synthetics. Use a combination of linear, planar, and volumetric elements. You need to have many elements in your construction to express the idea. Your construction should be abstract and emotionally expressive.

To generate ideas, think of some of these things and how you might express their essence in a visual form: electricity, communications, chemistry, construction equipment, travel (land, sea, air), music, circus, rodeo, dance, jazz, atomic power, theater, city. These are ideas that can elicit visual feelings. Use them to develop your own feeling for abstraction.

Do some loose two-dimensional sketches on large sheets of paper to get your ideas out. For example, think of the visual aspects of air transport—both the object and the implied motion. The plane coming up and going down. Then abstract it further. If you were thinking of a helicopter, you might do a series of hanging spirals over a flat surface. Pull the abstraction out and explore it.

Do some quick three-dimensional sketches in cardboard, wire, clay. The emotional content is here, and the objective is to capture it. Once captured, it exists in the exercise to be developed. The idea sketches should be an emotional reaction to the theme and a visual reaction that expresses shapes and movement.

"A design not only has to be structural, it has to appear to be structural. You have to get to recognize structure like you recognize a hot stove."

Search for the best overall proportions. Do some proportion studies of your three-dimensional sketches to find a successful proportion for the design as a whole.

Make a space sketch that establishes the first big tension between planes and volumes or groups of planes and volumes. The tensional relationship must strongly suggest or imply the proportions of the negative volume and establish a balance of directional forces from every position. It establishes the major theme that will hold the piece together. Once you have organized the way the elements sit in space, you can concentrate on the forms themselves.

WORKING IN FINAL MATERIALS:

Organize volumes, planes, and lines—in that order. Put together the elements of various materials in a pleasant relationship, using the principles from your previous learning. There are two major objectives here: maintaining the spirit of your idea and learning how to combine materials in a coherent whole.

Establish the dominant, subdominant, and subordinate elements. The dominant element should be beautiful in line and proportion, interesting in character, in the key position, and should express the movement demanded by the space sketch (that is, help the construction tell its story). The subdominant element should be beautiful in line and proportion and should complement the dominant.

Create the first big spatial relationship between the dominant and subdominant elements. This consists of two or three exciting movements that express the whole design and suggest the negative volume. (Be sure to place planes in two dimensions; don't line them up. Remember that spatial relationships consist of movements.)

"Rowena's suggestion of heavy equipment as an idea for the construction problem defined for me what industrial design might be about—that is, real things made up of many parts that all add up. At the time, a woman talking about these things made for an unusual association—like Marilyn Monroe talking physics."
— *Len Bacich*

"Rowena would say, 'Create a relationship at's worth the effort.'"
— *Lucia DeRespinis*

Refine the volumes, planes, and lines. Strengthen the spatial relationships and tensions between elements. Examine all lines in your design, including those created by planes. Ask how they relate to each other in space and position. In this problem, the relationship of surfaces to one another—the transition from one surface to another—is very important. In working with surfaces, you are learning how the eye moves across form and across space.

Establish a unity of all design elements and forces. Be sensitive to the joining of elements. There are two levels to this problem: the visual relationships and interconnections between elements, and how the elements flow.

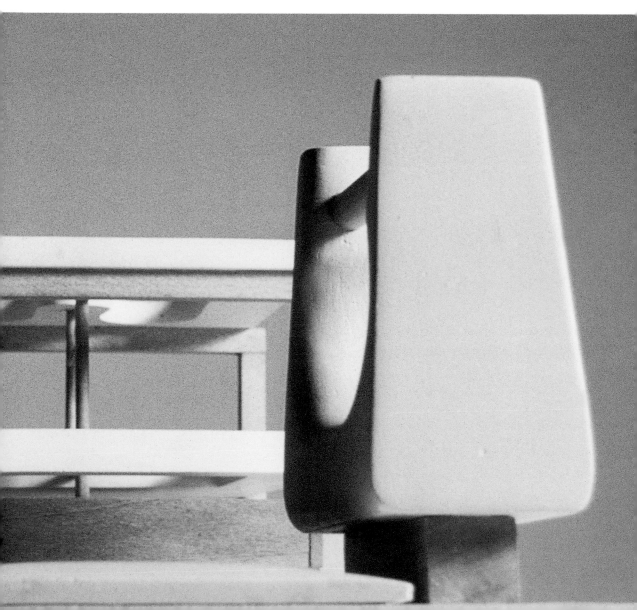

PROBLEM TWO: CONVEXITY

"The result of study with Miss
Reed was a marvelous insight
into the basics of twentieth-
century art in all its forms.
Nothing ever looked the same
after that year."
— *Doris Rosenquist*

"The exercises in convexity and concavity

are based on organic forms. They present

the opportunity to explore the properties

of a single, specific form. Unlike the

dramatic quality of the construction

exercise, the convexity and concavity

exercises deal with subtle gesture."

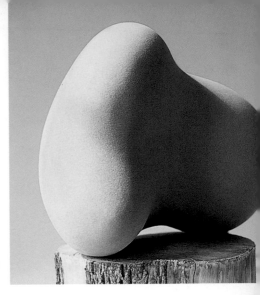

Here we undertake an exploration in depth of the subtle and involved relationships between the axes of large forms and the expanding planes of their surfaces, and the sensitive lines of the final configuration. This experience often leads to quite beautiful sculptural forms and can help you achieve a high degree of sensitivity and control of organic volumes. It is an excellent introduction to the problems faced in designing many of the common forms we live with: the telephone, the commode, and the automobile.

Convexity is the expression of positive volume or form pushing into negative space. (*Concavity* is the expression of negative space pushing into positive volume or form.) The characteristics of convexity are weight and bulk. We study convexity and concavity separately, and as we learn about one, we also learn about the other.

Our study of the relationship between the axis, the mass, and the outline is an exploration of how the mass creates surfaces and how the surfaces result in a silhouette. It's the opposite of defining volume the way you learned to do it in grade school. Conventionally, we define shape from the outside in by drawing the outline and filling in the space. This problem comes at it from the inside out. (Before you start, I suggest you acquire a copy of D'Arcy Thompson's book *Growth and Form*.)

Begin by making some sketches of organic forms in clay. Then quickly, with the flat side of a small piece of soft charcoal, make several large configuration sketches (one to a news sheet). Don't illustrate your three-dimensional sketches, but exaggerate or dramatize the qualities in them that you respond to. Use an interesting combination of curves. Stay at least ten feet away from your sketch, and do this from four different positions. The shapes (configuration) should not be too dramatic or the lines may become stylized and run away with the show.

"Always imagine these things one hundred times as large, and you'll see that the proportions make a huge difference."

Next, make some axis sketches using wires attached to planes, and play with configurations on the theme. Your axis sketches should be forceful, interesting, abstract, and asymmetrically balanced from every position. It should have an interesting gesture.

Now make two or more small clay space sketches reflecting your experience. Your sketches must have the quality of abstraction. This is true of any three-dimensional

design. They should emphasize character and movement. Don't become too concerned with outline. The outline changes with the evolution of the form, which pushes into space and expands at intervals.

The three-dimensional space sketches let you see the form in space and understand the relationships that space creates. They help you become aware of the negative space between the positive forms. The overall character and position of your form in space determines the most important tensional relationship. You can use these sketches to experiment by dramatizing certain overall or comparative proportions and grouping two or more volumes in opposition to other groups.

DEVELOP YOUR BEST THREE-DIMENSIONAL SKETCH.

Put your design together quickly and thoughtfully, stopping to look at it from a distance from time to time. Create a mass of two or three volumes using small blocks of clay, grouping forms into abstract shapes. Be aware of the contrast of forms. You should strive to express complementary contrast in proportion and in mass. Each form should improve the other, and the whole should be interesting three-dimensionally.

Establish the dominant-subdominant relationship. Then put subordinate relationships into place. (Remember that the dominant element is the most interesting shape and, nine times out of ten, is in the most prominent position.)

Work with the axes of the big volumes. Gesture, the movement of the axis, should be interesting and strong from every position. It is the core of the design. It keeps all other relationships (between plane, line, and space) in a state of suspension, tension, and balance. Axes should be balanced from every point of view and three-dimensional in concept. You should be able to feel the back of the volume from the front—that is, to feel the movement through the volume.

"The vocabulary was applicable to any design problem. The terms were principles that had to be contended with. It was, in a sense, very rigid— and yet very freeing."
— *Gerald Gulotta*

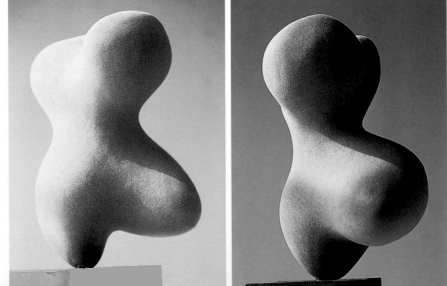

Keep in mind that in pure convexity, the eye is drawn around, over, and under. There is no hard-edged outline, no surfaces that meet at an angle. The negative space being resisted by form should flow around the volume. Your eye should be able to trace the way space flows always along the surface of protruding forms. Of course, there will be concavities, but keep them subtle, not deep.

You have three kinds of curves here: the curve of the axis, the curve of the planes going across the axis, and the curve of the configuration. They should all relate. Don't make curves parallel or perpendicular to the axes. It's much more subtle if you keep them on a diagonal.

Hold back the development of the planes that are diagonal to the axis. That is, hold back expansion except in character. Feel the mass first, then work on the planes and lines. Visualize the movement of forms. Be aware of surface tension.

"Things can get so big that the design outstrips the idea. There's a right size for every design—where it expresses the idea adequately and looks its best."

Do everything by carving. Work slowly or you'll make everything too small. Keep turning your work as you do it. Be careful not to spend so much time refining the shapes that you don't explore relationships.

For the final expression of the convexity problem, we work with a fifty-pound salt block. (Salt blocks are used on farms for livestock. They are about 12" x 12" but not true cubes. The salt block has a slight taper and a hole at one end for standing on a stick in the field.) Creating an organic form that does not retain the shape of the block adds to the challenge, but the material lends something to the experience. It is voluptuous, similar to marble. Unlike plaster, which is too fast, the salt block forces you to work more slowly.

Work the salt block with files and sandpaper. Never chip away at it. The process should be slow and careful. This will give you the opportunity to look very closely and learn to recognize the slightest changes in the form.

You should end up with a form that looks larger than the geometric form you started out with.

PROBLEM THREE: CONCAVITY

"The sculptural exercise that emphasizes

concavity explores a relationship that is

seldom understood. A talented and intuitive

designer may well arrive at sensitive,

positive volumes, but unless the important

relationship of the negative volumes, or

concavities, to the positive forms is

explored, his visual solution is only half

controlled. In the convexity exercise, you

were already learning about concavity—

about how negative volume affects form.

Now, the focus will be on concavity."

"The impression you got
from her teaching was
that she analyzed what
was wrong. Actually, she
saw that something was
or wasn't beautiful—and
then figured out why."
— *William Fogler*

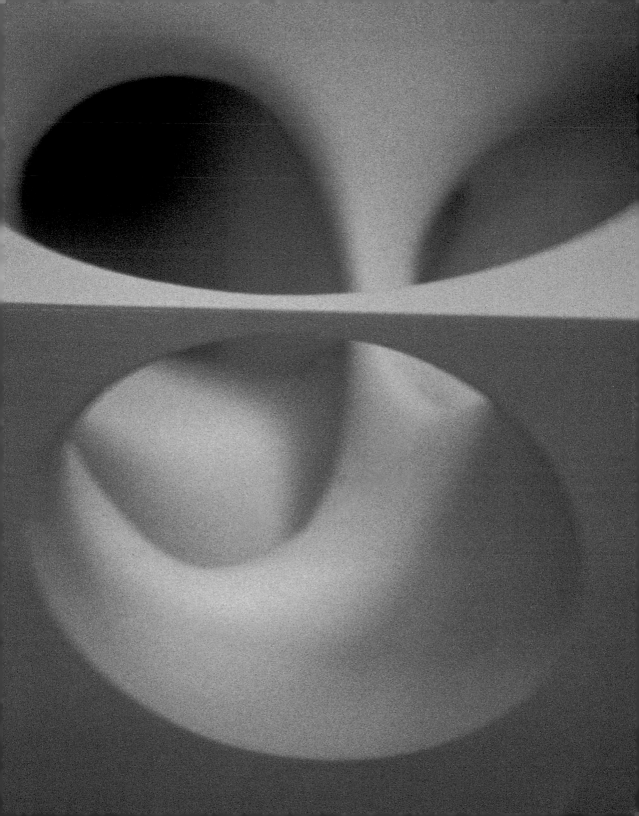

Think about natural elements and the slow erosion caused by wind and water. Make some clay sketches in which concavity establishes the character of the design. Design the surface of the concavity to contrast with the convexity.

"Good art or design rarely looks like it was done quickly. The artist or designer keeps working until all the parts of a painting, sculpture, or product relate to each other. That's what makes art last—regardless of its time. We respect it for its completion and its consistency."

Choose your most successful sketch and develop it. Use several blocks of clay and combine them. Decide whether you want a predominantly vertical or horizontal composition. Create shapes in which the character is interesting and the inherent and comparative proportions are pleasing.

Establish dominant, subdominant, and subordinate relationships. The first big spatial relationship should express the whole design. It should express the character and proportions of the volumes, the rhythmic movement of the volumes, and the variety and contrast of curved and straight lines.

Work on contrast. If things are different, they must complement each other. It's much harder to make things that are complementary than to make things that are the same. The complementary relationship must be understood from the very begin-

ning. If you're having trouble, just hang in there. Take one shape away, and see if it looks better without it.

Be aware of the axes. Not only do positive forms have axes, but concavities have axes as well. When the shape of a concavity is strong, it becomes a thing. It's almost like a positive form.

Do not trap the negative space. It should go around and come out and go someplace else. The space should flow, pushing against the volume in an eroding process, like a river through a canyon. Try to indicate how you'd go through it with the eye.

After you've gotten the volumes and the axes right, you can begin to play with one plane against another plane. Then you can play with all the other lines. See how the outside lines relate to the inside lines.

Execute your final design using a salt block or plaster block as your medium. Plaster is OK here. You can afford to work more quickly on the concavity exercise because you can gouge and hollow the material. If you work in salt, use files and sandpaper as you did in the convexity problem.

Although you're taking away material here, don't let your form contract like a prune becoming a raisin. You want to increase the presence of the form through its expansive characteristics. Once again, you want to end up with a form that looks larger than the geometric form you started out with.

"She was interested in Martha Graham's idea of dynamic tension across space: two figures doing something not at all the same but holding together. Like Graham in dance, Chanel in costume, and Calder in sculpture, she didn't see it as figures but as pure abstraction."

— *Len Bacich*

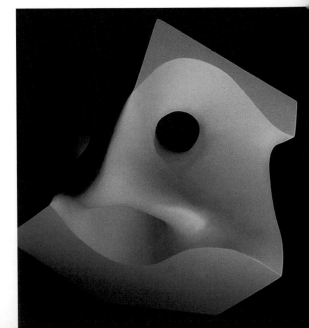

PART IV
STUDIES IN SPACE

"The objective of these space analysis

exercises is to develop your spatial

awareness and your ability to control and

use space as a design element.

I hope that through them you will become

accustomed to looking at space and

according space the same weight that

you do form."

PROBLEM ONE: SPACE ANALYSIS

"The study of planes in space is all about

relationships—about how the planes look

in relation to each other. The answer is

not *yes* or *no*—it's *yes* in relation to

something else or *no* in relation to

something else.

You will start by constructing space boxes: rectangles of whatever dimensions you choose. Starting with a sheet of foam core, cut a top, bottom, and three sides, and glue (or pin) them together. Make at least two boxes in exactly the same dimensions. One box will be your design box. The other will remain empty. It is the control against which you will measure your progress.

Now we introduce planes into the space. The goal is to create an organization that expands the negative volume. Using the axes of the planes and the tension between them, your challenge is to *enhance the awareness of the negative volume; activate the negative volume; make the overall organization as three-dimensional as possible.*

We will work with static, dynamic, and curvilinear planes, starting with the simplest and moving to the most complex. As the visual character of the planes becomes more complex, the exercise will require greater restraint, refinement, and subtlety, and you will find it more difficult to stay focused on our top priority, which is expanding the negative volume.

When you've created a successful organization, the negative volume in your design box should appear larger than in your control (empty) box. The careful positioning of planes and the tensional relationships beween them will give the negative volume a character of its own and make it come alive.

"Negative space was a tough concept for a seventeen-year-old. The understanding came later with some maturity."
— Bud Steinhelber

Regardless of the types of planes you're working with, the general rules for this space analysis experience are the same:

Planes should be complementary and should vary in character and proportion. Planes should be placed as three-dimensionally as possible, moving along the x, y, and z axes.

All planes must float. Use monofilament line or white thread to hang them. The planes should not pierce or touch each other or the box. (We don't deal with connections now because this would be distracting. To get hung up on them would distract your attention from the issue at hand, which is the negative volume of the space.)

Place the first plane with great consideration. It will establish the main movement in the space and set up a vibration that should affect how everything else works. The first plane really sets up the environment for designing in space. Place it, and then build on it.

Beware of the temptation to divide your box into symmetrical parts. To expand the space, you want to have a sense of volume, and as soon as you create a focused orientation point, you restrict that sense.

"Why do we concentrate so hard in these space boxes on expanding the negative volume? It's not because making space appear larger is necessarily the best thing to do, but it is the hardest thing to do. If you can do that, you can always make it smaller. The overall objective is to heighten your ability to use space as a design tool."

Establish dominant, subdominant, and subordinate relationships between planes and between spaces.

Make the planes aware of each other, and activate the spaces between them. Use the movements of the axes and the tensions among the surfaces of the planes to activate the space. Your two largest planes should really pull apart. It's not the planes themselves but the spatial tension between them that is the key to visual organization.

Be very careful never to allow the spaces between individual planes or groupings of planes to feel like separate spaces. They are all part of the whole. It's not just a matter of flow. It's a matter of unity.

"You'll find that you can gain better control of your design if you are aware of the abstract relationship between the axes. If I can impress that on you, I can almost retire. The axes create an abstraction in themselves that is very satisfactory. It's three-dimensional, there's opposition, there's balance, there's structure."

Don't lose sight of the whole. This exercise isn't about the forms of the planes. Concentrate on looking at all the planes within the box and their relationships to one another in terms of their impact on the negative volume. The planes should be aware of each other in proportion, character, and axis. Use this awareness to expand and activate the space.

It is hard to stay focused on the negative volume. We're used to concentrating on positive forms. It's a fine line we cross when the forms grab the attention and become more interesting than the negative space. It's more difficult to make the negative volume the most interesting thing. But the challenge is to do that—and to use forms that complement each other and are the appropriate size for the box.

After you've made a number of exploratory sketches, take the temperature of the boxes. (Think hot and cold.) Compare your design boxes with the empty box to see how successful you've been. You may find that within a single box, the temperature is higher in some places than in others. You just have to satisfy your eye, and feel it in your gut. It's like the first three-dimensional exercises. You have to persevere. If you spend a long time looking very critically, you will train your eye so that it responds to spatial relationships. This sensitivity will open up a whole new world.

As you work in new ideas, don't throw out the old. Keep them, and compare your new work with your old to see whether you're making progress. It's not unusual for students to have six boxes in the classroom: two empty, two original, and two revised.

"This calls for meditation and prayer—and proportion sketches."

"It takes five weeks to get students to look at what isn't there, five weeks of understanding what's happening to the space as a result of the positive forms."
— *Kate Hixon*

When you have completed your space box, ask yourself, **Have I expanded the negative volume?** Have I activated the negative volume? Is it just a construction of planes, or does the space have a life of its own? Have I achieved an interesting abstract organization? What is the dominant element, movement, gesture? Is there tension between the surfaces and the axes? Does the design look pleasing from all directions?

Finally, after telling you all this, I want to stress that the steps in the method and the techniques I've suggested aren't a bag of tricks. There are no tricks. Negative volume is an abstraction, and your task is to painstakingly find your own way to see it, feel it, and control it.

"My test of the negative volume is very literal. Pierce it, and it should say, 'ouch!'"

STATIC PLANES

In the first problem, we work with a minimum of three planes, all cut from foam core of the same thickness and all with ninety-degree corners. The proportions of the planes are up to you. In this exercise using static planes, all planes must be parallel or at right angles to each other and to the box. Arrange the planes in your design box following the rules we've discussed, which apply to all of the space analysis exercises—static, dynamic, and curvilinear.

Don't forget to work with planes moving along all three (x, y, and z) axes.

Never put a plane down the middle of your space. In a static box, the cross it creates with the edges of the box will distract the eye from the space you're trying to activate.

When you have succeeded in expanding the total negative volume in your white box, you will add gray value. Use a minimum of three gray values, with two steps between each on the color chart. The gray can be placed on any surface—on the top, bottom, or sides of the box; on planes; or on edges. It is not meant to be decorative. Its purpose is to add complexity, to create additional tensions (between gray values as well as between shapes) that expand the negative volume and make your gray box look larger than your white one.

Be selective in your use of gray values. If you use them on all of your planes, you'll begin to lose the sensation of space, and the planes will become a graphic presentation of your idea. Remember that in this exercise, you want to force the eye to see the space created by the placement of planes, not just to see the planes themselves.

After you have gained some experience in using gray values to expand the negative volume, experiment with color. You may use as many colors as you choose or one color in many values. Apply them to any surface, but do it in a disciplined way. Don't create poster solutions; your goal is to use the energy of the color to expand the negative volume.

"Negative space brings all the parts together. It provides the fullness. The space has form and proportion, and for the most part, it's much more complex than the positive forms you're working with. But you can't grab it. You have to learn to see it."

— *Debera Johnso*

DYNAMIC PLANES

In this exercise, we are working with dynamic (tapered) planes, which should not have right angles or triangular (arrowhead) tips and are never positioned at right angles to other planes or to the top, bottom, or sides of your box. Once again, the planes should not pierce or connect with each other. You may use complex planes—that is, planes that change direction—but each such plane must be a single bent plane, not two connected planes.

If you decide to work with simple planes, use three. You can use only two if you include complex planes in your design. Don't forget to work with planes moving along all three (x, y, and z) axes, and with these dynamic planes, along all axes in between.

"The design of the axes is the design of almost anything."

You will find that the way planes are cut is important. Dynamic planes must be tapered. A plane cut on the table may look quite different inside the space box. Design the planes in the context of the box. Start with a tapered plane, hold it up inside the box, and cut the edges to reinforce the axis, always paying attention to the relative proportion, character, and complementary relationships between planes.

In this experience with dynamic planes, the movement of the axes is the top priority. Position the planes so that you become aware of the axes, so that you create tension between the axes of the planes.

Remember not to divide your box into symmetrical parts. Just as you need to be careful not to cut your static box in two or four, you need to guard against bisecting your dynamic box along the diagonal.

As in the static spaces, you must establish dominant, subdominant, and subordinate relationships. The dominant and subdominant together should constitute more than half of the balance of directional forces, leaving room for completing the balance with some smaller shapes.

The largest plane should be the most dramatic, the most visually structural, and should have an axis that sets up vibrations in the whole box. Once you get that, you can think of the other planes. I can't emphasize enough how important your first move in the box is. It can make or break it.

Now focus on the axes. Start with a tapered plane. Use sixteenth-inch black charting tape to mark the axes of the planes. Analyze the lines made by the tape. Do the planes support the movement of the axes or distract the eye and draw it to their edges?

The relationship among the axes of the planes is the most crucial relationship in this exercise. Do not allow the outlines of the planes to become more important than the axes. (Never do that in any art form.) Making the outline stronger or more interesting than the axes weakens the design. It flattens space, making it graphic instead of three-dimensional. You end up seeing the line instead of the thrust; and if you're looking at the outline, you don't see the volume.

The problem of dynamic planes in space includes all the challenges of the static problem, plus it adds speed to the equation, which will make you aware of the importance of structure. The organization of planes should be visually structural. A plane moving across space can't be too heavy or it will look like it's going to fall down. Think of how an airplane changes direction in space, how it banks as it slows down. Don't create planes that appear to be clouds floating in the atmosphere. Create an organization in which the planes look like they are structurally comfortable. Choose a gesture that's appropriate to the situation. (It's inappropriate for a hippo to do a pirouette.)

"Buckminster Fuller's engineer called her space boxes 'fantasy architecture.' What she was doing were abstractions of the things in the space—great big sweeps that go through a room—which the artist and designer can control if they're aware."

— *Robert Kolli*

You'll discover that a plane that looks fine in one box won't necessarily look like it can sustain the same speed in a box of different proportions because of the space around it. Tapering a plane will increase its speed.

The tensions among dynamic planes are more complicated than in the static situation. You have two kinds of tension in this exercise: the tension between the surfaces of the planes and the tension between the axes. You have to make those two forces create the abstract organization. Meanwhile, you must continue trying to activate the negative volume. It's getting harder and harder.

In this problem, you experience how the balance of directional forces, the speed of the axes, and the tension among the planes relate to the space around them. You begin to see how the space between planes is activated. Space takes on a heightened sense of energy. It plays an active role in the design. The space is actually pushing against the surfaces of the planes.

CURVILINEAR PLANES

Finally, we work with curvilinear planes. First, for a warm-up, refer to the curve chart you created for the wire problem. The vocabulary of curves is the same whether you're working with lines or planes. This is the vocabulary you will work with here.

In order to be able to make the curved planes, you'll need to switch your material from foam core to bristol board. Be aware of the importance of taking the axes all

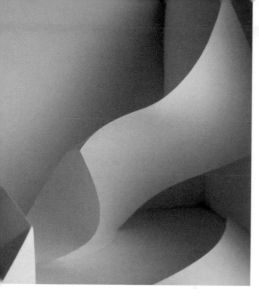

the way through your planes. The shape of the plane should reflect where the movement starts and where it is going.

Start with a tapered plane and curve it. Hold the plane in space, and tape the axis. Note that the edge doesn't do what the curve is doing. You will discover that the edges must be trimmed to make the movement of the plane clear. Don't radius the edges of the plane. Your planes shouldn't look like Fritos.

Use two or more planes. If you use only two, one must be a complex curve (a curve that is a combination of two curves, like a reverse curve) to ensure that you move in all three directions. Position the curves in your box to move through space in the most interesting ways you can. If you are working with more than three planes, create groupings.

Follow the guidelines for all the space analysis exercises, beginning by establishing dominant, subdominant, and subordinate relationships. Once again, don't let your planes touch or pierce each other. Crafting your design will be more difficult in the curvilinear space analysis exercise than in the static or dynamic. You may need up to six hanging points for each plane to make it work.

Remember that you have three challenges in this problem. First, expand the space, and activate the negative volume. Second, establish unity of the entire space. And third, create a design in which space and form are equally important and so interdependent that they cannot be separated.

As with dynamic planes, when working with curvilinear planes, you should also be aware of speed. Analyze your curved planes in terms of speed. Ask yourself how fast the curves of the planes must be moving for the planes to sustain their positions in your design.

This exercise requires restraint and subtlety. There's a temptation to create axes that roll and then become objects in space instead of movements.

Curvilinear planes can be very interesting shapes. It's tempting to concentrate on them and forget the space. Students often work hard to put something beautiful inside the box, but they forget about the box itself. They create objects in a box instead of space. The two must be inextricably linked. The design shouldn't be able to live without the box or the box without the design.

"Students think there's a trick involved, like false perspective. You can trick the eye into seeing a space as deeper than it is, but that has nothing to do with volume. The space will also look narrower. What you're striving for here is a sense of expanding the total volume of the space. It's a matter of sensitizing the eye to what's alive in the space."

— *Kate Hixon*

PROBLEM TWO: SPACE DESIGN

" This project follows the abstract

exercises in space analysis and cannot be

successfully completed until the student

has mastered those exercises."

We start by making some three-dimensional sketches of an interesting space, interior or exterior. Use cardboard, foam core, bristol board, bottle caps—any materials that lend themselves to the expression of your idea. Don't think about a specific application at this stage. Just use this opportunity for exploration.

Choose any subject you think you can control as long as it's something that really excites you. You're going to be dealing here with the emotional qualities of space so you must be able to communicate feeling within the space. It might be a static, dynamic, or organic space, or a combination of the three. In this project, you will be emphasizing positive forms more than you have until now. Your project should be a ratio of about sixty percent space organization to forty percent positive form, or vice versa.

"You have no business putting in the detail until you have the space solved. In nine times out of ten, the designers of interior spaces focus so much on forms and color that they literally fill the space up, and the space they started with disappears. That's why this exercise is so important."

I hope you'll select a subject that's imaginative, dramatic, and stimulating. Something that draws on the experiences you've been having, not some ordinary interior project that any interior designer could do. Don't choose something that's purely functional. A swimming pool, gymnasium, and zoo are interesting ideas that students before you have explored. Or you might consider a gallery, a chapel, a theater, a stadium, an open-air market. Keep your three-dimensional idea sketches abstract. Work quickly and intuitively.

Choose six of your three-dimensional sketches, and make them better. Work on the relationships of elements and the movements in space. When you have achieved a refined sketch that interests you and has real promise, then consider the implications of your decision. Why do certain forms have the shape they have, and how do they relate to other forms and to the total space?

"Stop thinking about objects! Don't call it a 'table.' Call it a 'plane.' How this plane relates to that plane. Talking this way helps you to think."

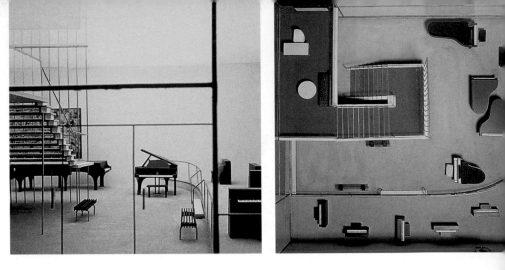

"Rowena believed that if you could do the space analysis properly, it proved that you could handle anything. It was a holistic view of the world. The culminating architectural problem was a way of bringing the whole thing together."

— *Bruce Hannah*

Next, make some two-dimensional proportion sketches. Use newsprint and Conte Crayon to make quick, plan-view sketches in which you analyze proportion and gesture. These sketches are only for analysis. Don't treat them as drafting.

Continue working on your sketch, gradually introducing more functionality but focusing still on the abstraction.

You need not address real-world restrictions like cost. In the real world, you'll be designing to a brief. In this experience, think of abstraction as your only brief. Here's your chance to design a magnificent, long cantilever that few people would be willing to pay for.

Small forms, which can be anything from furniture to staircases to art objects, are crucial in this exercise. You will need to create forms of appropriate scale, proportion, and gesture to relate to the space. Be aware that a group of small forms can create a spatial element. For example, rows of stadium seating can become a large plane.

Don't get caught up too early in your design with these forms. Solve the big spatial problem first, then integrate the small forms into the space. Work out the details in your final model.

"The most difficult part of doing the interior project was to work from the abstract—to remember that tables and chairs are horizontal planes and a staircase is a diagonal plane. As a professional, it's so easy to get drawn into technical issues and fabrication problems, and give the design away. You can have both."

— *Pamela Waters*

PART V
DEVELOPMENT

"These are examples of more advanced work,

in which students continue to explore

abstract forms but also begin to apply some

practical criteria to their work. They are not

meant to be real products or spaces; rather,

they demonstrate the stage between purely

formal exercises and real products designed

for production. In these examples, students

apply functional, ergonomic, and material

requirements along with form-making skills

without having these requirements

dominate the creative process."

"She taught me to question everything. She taught me the difference between a bland, boring design and something that has significant and exciting aesthetic value."

— *Frank Grunwald*

Some of these solutions directly reflect earlier abstract exercises. For example, the first telephone shown on the previous page employs rather direct combinations of line (the handset), plane (the tapering neck of the cradle arm), and volume (the base) with the volume of the base clearly derived from the exploration of convexity and concavity. Its form harks back to early freestanding models in which the handset hangs (and from which we derive the reference to "hanging up" the phone).

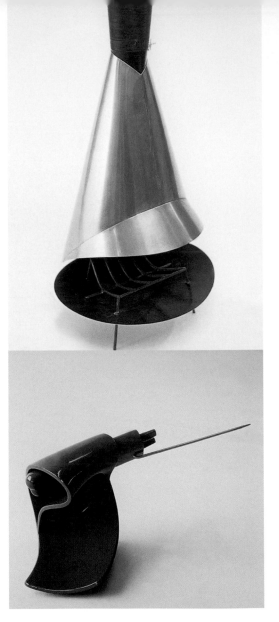

Some of the work employs form to suggest function or effect. For example, the curved planes that form the body of the drill and the gesture created by the concavity in its side suggest what this tool does. One can almost see wood or metal curling as the drill does its work. The radio is a complex consideration of the elements of line, plane, and volume in which the thrust of the plane creates a strong sense of motion and also creates a relationship between the form of the object and the sound it is designed to transmit. The electric drill is a bold construction in which the mass and gesture of the volumes suggest power. One project included here rethinks function-as-usual. The designer of the movie projector (see page 144) thought about the tool in the hands of the projectionist: orienting the object horizontally allows the person running the machine to see the screen even when changing reels.

"The exercises developed my hand and my mind. I don't think about it all the time. I just do it."

— Lisa Smith

In some of these solutions, form is derived from the possibilities of materials and production processes. The flowing movement of the surfaces on the car (a project from the early 1960s), the continuous form of the back as it drops into the interior, and the concavity behind the wheel, which offers a variation on the usual cutout solution, suggest formed-and-molded rather than cut-and-welded production.

The group of phones (see page 144) illustrates the variety of formal approaches (concave and convex volumes, rectilinear and planar volumes) and functional solutions (dials and push but-

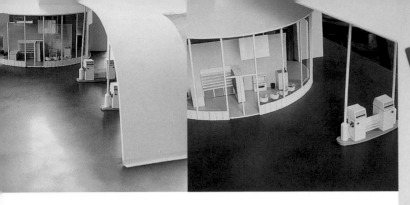

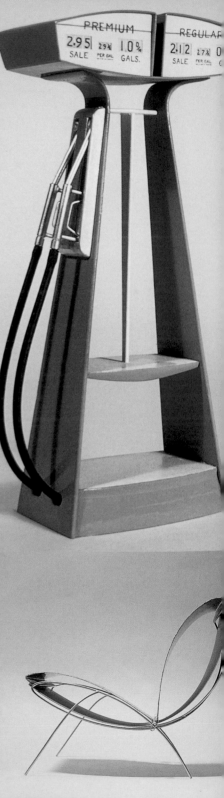

tons) that can be brought to bear on the same problem. The turntable with cassette recorder considers design for new technology. Cassettes were a recent innovation at the time this project was completed.

"If you can't make it more beautiful, what's the point? Almost anybody can do it the other way."

The design for a gas station creates functional space within a space.

The chairs employ a variety of materials to achieve radically different results: planes in tension, pinching and expanding to create volumetric form; curved planes creating negative volume in a design that is all about gesture and proportion; and metal tubing that outlines an elegant linear path.

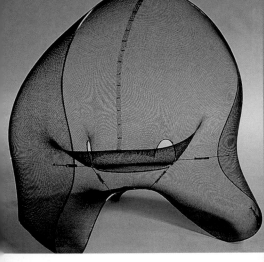

"If you're ever in a bind in a design project—whether it's a car or any other product— you can get yourself off dead center by thinking dominant-subdominant-subordinate. It's the backbone of design."

"The most important gift
she gave was the ability
to create a sense of unity.
The recognition that if
you take away one piece,
the design falls apart. It's
a tool you can use
forever, and it grows and
grows if you allow it to."
— *Jeff Kapec*

PART V
PROFESSIONAL WORK

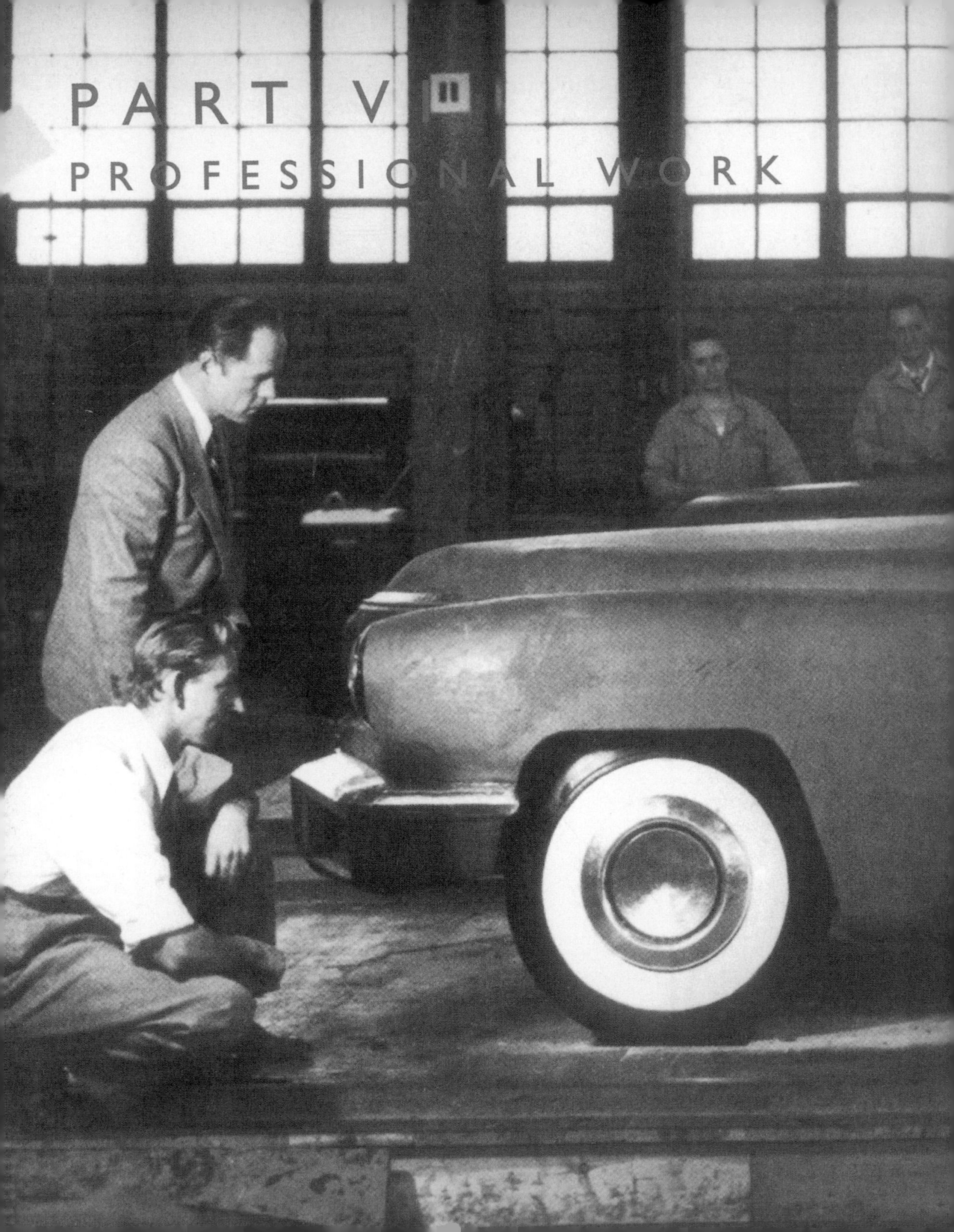

Tucker

Selected professional work by Rowena Reed's students—products, packaging, furniture, lighting, automobiles, jewelry, interiors, exhibitions, and sculpture—that reflect the expression of abstract visual relationships in finished form and materials.

Tucker advanced '52 model,
1947. From the left: Budd
Steinhilber, Hal Bergstrom,
Philip Egan, and Walter
Margulies (other Lippencott
designers not shown: Read
Viemeister and Tucker
Madawick)

DAP (logo and packaging)
Read Viemeister
and Budd Steinhilber
Vie Design Studios
1951

"Her teaching worked by
osmosis and verifying
what she told us through
experience. We absorbed
it while not realizing it,
then understood the
validity of it later on."
— *Read Viemeister*

Igloo
Playmate cooler
M. Polhemus

Trimline phone
Don M. Genaro at Henry Dreyfuss Associates for AT&T, 1964

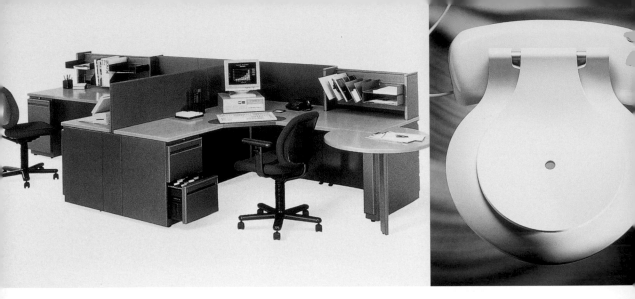

Hannah desk
Bruce Hannah for Knoll
1990

Zöe Washlet toilet seat
Ayse Birsel for Toto
1995

OXO GoodGrips
Davin Stowell, Tucker Viemeister, and Michael Calahanat
Smart Design
1990

Pollock chair
Charles Pollock for Knoll
1965

Pod earrings
Ted Meuhling
1984

Cities Service gas station
Don M. Genaro
1960

Citröen-N2
(proposal)
Carl L. Olsen
1986

Hall of Faces
Holocaust Museum
Washington, D.C.
Ralph Appelbaum
1993

Nambé spiral candle holders
Linda Celentano and Lisa Smith
1999

Accesories tape dispenser
Bruce Hannah and Ayse Birsel for Knoll
1990

Black & Decker
Cordless grass shears
Robert Somers

"The artist is primarily a visual person. I have always believed that there is no essential difference between the basic visual relationships that concern the fine artist, the graphic artist, the industrial designer, and the architect. The difference is in the degree of complexity of visual organization demanded by each situation. Beyond that, there are the materials and techniques of each area. I am convinced that there is a visual discipline suitable for all of these areas....It is [based on] the exciting concept that there can be order and structure to the organization of visual expression."

This book began as an NEA grant to Rowena Reed in 1982. Thanks to

a dedicated band of her students and colleagues, it's finally published.

It was designed by Tucker Viemeister and

Seth Kornfeld; undoubtedly, she would

have made some changes.

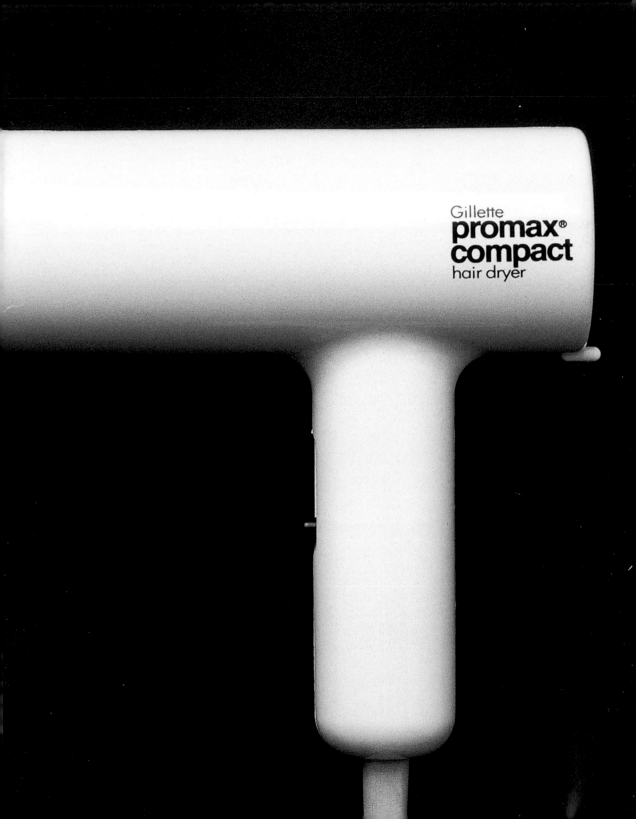

Transition porcelain dinnerware
Gerald Gulotta
Block China Corporation
1967

Arch flatware
George Schmidt for Cuisine Cookware

Korean War
Veterans Memorial
Louis Nelson
1995

Cuisinart
Mark Harrison
1978

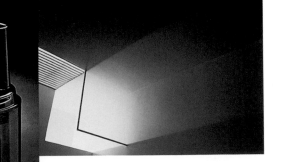

Light Form
Peter Barna
1990

Gillette Promax compact hair dryer
Morison Cousins and Michael Cousins
1978